BERKSHIl__
CRICKETERS
1844-2008

compiled by

Tony Percival

Published by the Association of Cricket Statisticians and Historians, Cardiff CF11 9XR
2008
Typeset by Limlow Books
Printed by City Press, Leeds
ISBN: 978 1 905138 70 8

Berkshire 2008

standing: **D Morris** (*team manager*), **CD Crowe, D Barnes, S Naylor, J Trower, R Johnson, J McLean, T Dellor** (*coach*),
Mrs S Jones (*scorer*), **R New** (*Hon Secretary*)

front: **N Denning, T Lambert, M Stokes, B Mordt** (*captain*), **J Morris, P Carter, CP Crowe**

(photo: Peter Bloodworth/Reading Evening Post)

INTRODUCTION

Cricket spread quickly throughout Berkshire in the 18th century with matches being reported in towns such as Bray, Longworth, Reading, Sonning, Tilehurst and Wokingham. As early as 1748 London beat Berkshire, 5 a side, and in 1769 Surrey beat Berkshire on Datchet Common although it is not known if a properly constituted County Club actually existed. There are subsequently regular newspaper references to Berkshire playing other counties and MCC.

However, in the mid 1800s it is possible that there may have been a County Club in existence as, according to Rowland Bowen, there was a report in *Bell's Life* on the Club's AGM on 4th May 1841 with no indication it was a new Club formation. There have been matches traced spasmodically between 1844 and 1872 and where the scores are available the players have been included with their averages in the first section. It is not been possible, however, to trace if the Club was in continuous existence throughout the period, although it could have been reformed around 1856. Opponents in this period included Sussex, Kent, Hampshire, Wiltshire.

The present County Club was formed on 12th March 1895 with HRH Prince Christian as the Club's first President. It was advocated that the county ground should be at Reading. The Club has been in continuous existence since and entered the Minor Counties Championship from 1896, although it played two matches in 1895 against counties playing in the Championship. The main opponents over the years were Buckinghamshire, Devon, Dorset, Oxfordshire and Wiltshire. On the revision of the Championship in 1983 when it was divided into two divisions, East and West, Berkshire was put in the Western Division and opponents subsequently have been Cheshire, Cornwall, Devon, Dorset, Herefordshire (who replaced Buckinghamshire in 1992), Oxfordshire, Shropshire, Wales (who replaced Somerset II in 1988) and Wiltshire. After the formation most home matches were played at the County Ground, Kensington Road, Reading until 1939, but after WWII home matches have been played at various grounds throughout the County.

Prior to 2008 the County has only had limited success winning the Minor Counties Championship in 1924, 1928 and 1953, and the Knock Out Cup once, in 2004. However, in 2008 the County won the Minor Counties Championship and was the beaten KO finalist.

I wish to thank Roy New the Berkshire Secretary for his substantial input in tracing and providing scorecards and obtaining player's details. I have also been given help by Roger Heavens, Julian Lawton Smith and as always by Don Ambrose to which I am again extremely grateful. I also am indebted to Tony Webb who has been an inspiration again and has readily supplied me with endless detail now for some years. Kevin Preston has kindly provided the information on players appearing in Minor Counties representative matches. Peter Wynne Thomas, Peter Griffiths, Philip Bailey, David Morris and many former and current players and officials have also provided me with information and once again their help is much appreciated.

I also wish to thank Peter Griffiths and *CricketArchive* for providing the averages, which has substantially reduced the time needed to compile the book. Unfortunately due to large gaps in the availability of the official scorebooks, scores have had to be taken from newspapers and these inevitably have not always been accurate. The averages for the period 1895-2008 do not include friendly matches but relate to Championship matches only.

In the earlier period a start date for the biographies has been taken as 1844 as in earlier matches many of the players were shown without initials, making identification almost impossible, and in some instances summary scores only could be traced. Also that year was the first recorded County matches after a possible County Club formation in the early 1840's.

The matches taken into consideration 1844-72 were:

v Buckinghamshire	1-2 August 1844
	7 August 1846
	10 September 1849
	18 September 1849
	13 August 1857
v Oxfordshire	22-23 August 1853
v Wiltshire	28 June 1858
	28 June 1859
v Sussex	22-23 June 1858
	16-17 August 1858
	14-15 July 1859
	15-17 August 1859
	9-10 July 1860
	30 July-1 August 1860
v Kent	12 August 1859
	16 July 1860
v Hampshire	10-11 August 1860
	9-10 August 1869
	8-9 August 1870
	5-6 August 1872
v Eton College	12 July 1856
	16 July 1859
v Gentlemen of England	7 August 1858

Tony Percival
December 2008

Notes

b	born (where abbreviation is shown, eg 3Q, this indicates the quarter in which birth registered with Registrar of Births.)
c	christened
d	died
ed	Educated
C	College
GS	Grammar School
HS	High School
P	Polytechnic
SFC	Sixth Form College
SS	Secondary School
TC	Technical College
U	University
UAU	University Athletic Union
UCCE	University College of Cricketing Excellence
YC	Young Cricketer

England (1)	Number of Test Matches for England (similarly with other countries)
CU	Cambridge University (with number of years obtained blue in brackets)
OU	Oxford University (with number of years obtained blue in brackets)
CB	Cricket Board
ESCA	Represented English Schools Cricket Association under-19s
NAYC	National Association of Young Cricketers
Cap	Awarded County Cap followed by year

The details of a player's appearances for the Minor Counties Cricket Association representative XIs have been shown separately for each type of match as follows:

fc	first-class
sc	second class (not defined as first-class i.e. mainly 2-day matches)
BHC	Benson and Hedges Cup
u-25	Under-25 matches in Bain Hogg/Aon/Second XI Trophy
lo	Limited overs matches
odm	other one day matches, not limited overs

Types of batsman/bowler are the standard accepted abbreviations.

The counties have only been shown after places of birth and death when other than Berkshire.

The Club shown after the player's name is the Club he was playing at when representing Berkshire. In the earlier years, however, it has not always been possible to confirm this information although it is known the player had played for the Club listed.

The Compiler would appreciate receiving information to assist in completing any missing details of players. His address is 31 Covert Rise, Tattenhall, Cheshire CH3 9HA. You can e-mail him at tony@tonyandsue.demon.co.uk

Notes On Career Records

It has not been possible to obtain full bowling analyses in early nineteenth century matches.

BERKSHIRE CRICKETERS 1844-1872

AUSTEN-LEIGH, AUGUSTUS (1858-70). b 17.7.1840 Scarlets. d 28.1.1905 Cambridge. ed Eton; CU (King's). wk. Brother of A.H., C., C.E., E.C., W. and S.A.Leigh. Club: Maidenhead.

AUSTEN-LEIGH, Rev. ARTHUR HENRY (1857-72). b 28.2.1836 Speen, Newbury. d 29.7.1917 Reading. ed Cheltenham; OU (St John's). Brother of A., C., C.E., E.C., W. and S.A.Leigh. Club: Maidenhead.

AUSTEN-LEIGH, CHOLMELEY (1856-60). b 26.9.1829 Tring, Hertfordshire. d 30.9.1899 Kingston upon Thames, Surrey. ed OU (Balliol, Trinity). Brother of A., A.H., C.E., E.C., W. and S.A.Leigh. Club: Maidenhead.

AUSTEN-LEIGH, CHARLES EDWARD (1857-60). b 30.6.1832 Tring, Hertfordshire. d 17.11.1924 Berwick Station, Sussex. ed Winchester; Harrow; OU (Balliol). Brother of A., A.H., C., E.C., W. and S.A.Leigh. Club: Maidenhead.

AUSTEN-LEIGH, EDWARD COMPTON (1857-72). b 1.5.1839 Scarlets. d 4.3.1916 Colenorton, Eton College. ed Eton; CU (King's). Tennis (Blue). Brother of A., A.H., C., C.E., W. and S.A.Leigh. Club: Maidenhead.

AUSTEN-LEIGH, WILLIAM (1860-69). b 11.5.1843 Scarlets. d 27.11.1921 Roehampton, London. Brother of A., A.H., C., C.E., E.C. and S.A.Leigh. Club: Maidenhead.

BACON, WILLIAM (1849). b 28.7.1815 Oxford. d 1Q.1882 Thame, Oxfordshire. Professional. Club: Cowley.

BARKER, Rev. ALFRED GRESLEY (1858-59). b 11.12.1835 Bloomsbury, London. d 20.11.1906 Sherfield on Loddon, Hampshire. ed OU (Trinity). Brother of G.W. Clubs: Reading, Hungerford Park, Maidenhead.

BARKER, GEORGE WILLIAM (1856-59). b 8.8.1831 Stanlake Park. d 10.9.1869 Stanlake Park. ed Rugby; OU (Christ Church). Brother of A.G.

BEALE, ALEXANDER (1858). c 15.2.1826 Blandford Forum, Dorset. d 4.3.1907 Reading. Club: Reading.

BEECH (1849).

BOOTH, HENRY WILLIAM (1853-56). b 27.4.1815 Roydon House, Essex. d 7.8.1883 Chiswick, Middlesex. ed Eton; CU (Christ's). Also CU (1), Hertfordshire. Club: Hungerford Park.

BOWLES, Captain RICHARD FRANCIS (1853). c 22.6.1828 Milton. d 16.8.1916 Wallingford. ed OU (Exeter). Club: Reading.

BURRIN, DAVID (1857). b 1.3.1829 Cowley, Oxfordshire. d 2Q.1863 Headington, Oxfordshire. Also Buckinghamshire. Professional. Clubs: Cowley, Reading.

CARTER, Rev. THOMAS GARDEN (1846-49). c 8.10.1823 Croydon, Surrey. d 6.12.1885 Linton, Kent. ed Eton; CU (Trinity).

CLEAVE, JOHN (1844-49). b 1811 Windsor. d 4Q.1881 Windsor. Club: Windsor and Eton.

COLERIDGE, ALFRED JAMES (1856). c 19.12.1831 Eton, Buckinghamshire. d 8.3.1880 Bedford. ed Eton; OU (Magdalene and University). Club: Maidenhead.

COLLINS, CLIFTON WILBRAHAM (1869-70). b 5.5.1844 Clifton Hampden, Oxfordshire. d 25.9.1918.Cambridge. ed OU (Magdalene). Club: Reading.

CRAIGIE (1860).

CROFT, S. (1846).

CROWDER, FREDERICK (1869). b 8.10.1845 Marylebone, London. d 27.3.1938 Oxford. ed Rugby; OU (Brasennose). Rowing (OU (2)). Club: Reading.

CROWDY, Rev. JAMES GORDON (1869-70). b 2.7.1847 Westrop House, Highworth, Wiltshire. d 16.12.1918 Sarum, Winchester, Hampshire. ed Rugby; OU (Wadham). rhb. Also Hampshire, Worcestershire, Devon.

DORRINTON, WILLIAM (1844). b 29.4.1809 West Malling, Kent. d 8.11.1848 West Malling, Kent. rhb. wk. Also Kent, Hampshire, Suffolk. Son of Thomas (Kent), brother of Alban (Kent). Professional. Club: MCC (ground bowler).

DUPUIS, GEORGE RICHARD (1856). b 23.3.1835 Eton, Buckinghamshire. d 30.1.1912 Sessay Hall, Thirsk, Yorkshire. ed Eton; CU (King's). Also CU (1), Buckinghamshire. Father of F.J. (Staffordshire), nephew of H. (OU). Club: Maidenhead.

EVERETT, Rev. CHARLES HENRY (1853-60). b 1835 Chiddingfold, Surrey. d 15.1.1896 Sidmouth, Devon. ed OU (Balliol). Also Hampshire. Brother-in-law of H.Stewart (Hampshire) and W.A.Stewart (OU, Hampshire). Club: Hungerford Park.

EVERETT, FREDERICK (1858-60). b 3Q.1838 Everley Pewsey, Wiltshire. d 2Q.1904 Auckland, Durham. ed Royal Agricultural C. Club: Hungerford Park

EYRE, FRANCIS GEORGE (1858-59). b 18.8.1840 Englefield. d 22.1.1861 St Leonard's-on-Sea, Sussex. ed Winchester; OU (University).

FANNING, EDWARD (1869). b 16.3.1848 Sydney, New South Wales, Australia. d 30.11.1917 St Kilda, Melbourne, Victoria, Australia. ed OU (Trinity). Also Victoria.

FITZGERALD, ROBERT ALLAN (1858-59). b 1.10.1834 Purley House. d 28.10.1881 Chorley Wood, Hertfordshire. ed Harrow; CU (Trinity) Also CU (2), Middlesex, Ireland, Hertfordshire, Buckinghamshire. rhb. rfr. Tour: Fitzgerald to North America. Honorary Secretary MCC (1863-76). Brother of A.W. (MCC), brother-in-law of E.C.Leigh. Club: Hungerford Park.

FORBES, WILLIAM ASHBURNER (1846). b 1826 Sunninghill. d 21.5.1897 Tunbridge Wells, Kent. Club: Maidenhead.

GIBBS, GEORGE HENRY (1860). b 2Q.1843 Hungerford.

GIBBS, J. (1860).

GODDARD, T. (1849). Club: Reading.

GOODALL, WILLIAM (1846). b 1.10.1831 St Pancras, London. Ed Eton; CU (Clare).

GOODCHILD (1844). Club: Windsor and Eton.

GOODLAKE, Major GERALD LITTLEHALES V.C. (1858). b 14.5.1832 Faringdon. d 5.4.1890 Denham, Middlesex. ed Eton. Club: Coldstream Guards.

GRAHAM, CHARLES ARTHUR (1853). b 1832 Newbury. Club: Hungerford Park.

GRAHAM, G. (1853). Club: Hungerford Park.

GRAHAM, W. (1853).

GRANTHAM (1849).

GREEN, J. (1849). Club: Reading.

HARDING, J. (1849).

HAYGARTH, EDWARD BROWNLOW (1870-72). b 26.4.1854 Cirencester, Gloucestershire. d 14.4.1915 Siddington Manor, Gloucestershire. ed Lancing. rhb. u. wk. Also Hampshire, Gloucestershire. Football (England). Brother of J.W., cousin of A. (Middlesex and Surrey), uncle of F.H.Gresson (Sussex).

HAYGARTH, JOHN WILLIAM (1872). b 3.12.1842 Rodmarton, Gloucestershire. d 30.3.1923 Boonah, Queensland, Australia. ed Winchester; OU (Corpus). rhb. wk. Also OU (3), Gloucestershire. Brother of E.B., cousin of A. (Middlesex and Sussex), uncle of F.H.Gresson (Sussex).

HAYWARD, GEORGE (1860-72). b 1838 Long Wittenham. d 2Q.1880 Wallingford. Club: Reading.

HOMEWOOD, W. (1860).

HUNTER, Sir CLAUDIUS STEPHEN PAUL (1859). c 1.12.1825 Ghazeepore, India. d 7.1.1890 Mortimer Hill, Bradfield. ed Eton; OU (St John's).

HUNTER, HENRY LANNOY (1869). b 17.9.1836 Beech Hill, Reading. d 12.9.1909 Beech Hill, Reading. ed Eton; OU (Christ Church). Also Hampshire Gentlemen. Club: Reading.

JOLLYE, Rev. HENRY CLARKE (1870). b 10.1841 Broome, Norfolk. d 17.12.1902 Walton, Wiltshire. ed Bradfield; OU (Lincoln).

KITSON, Rev. FRANCIS JOHN (1853). b 1811 Denbury, Devon. d 28.1.1891 Bath, Somerset. ed OU (St John's).

LAWRENCE (1849).

LEDIARD, PEREGRINE (1849). b 1813 Bristol, Gloucestershire. d 8.8.1892 Marylebone, London. Club: Reading.

LEE, Rev. ARTHUR GEORGE (1869-72). b 31.8.1849 Chelsea, London. d 11.7.1925 Paddington, London. ed Westminster; OU (Worcester, Univ Coll, St Alban Hall). rhb. wk. Also OU, Worcestershire, Suffolk. Brother of F.H.

LEE, FREDERIC HUGH (1872). b 14.9.1855 Chelsea, London. d 6.2.1924 Aberdeen. ed Marlborough: OU (Trinity). Also Suffolk. Brother of A.G.

LEIGH, Hon. Sir EDWARD CHANDOS (1856). b 22.12.1832 Stoneleigh Abbey, Kenilworth, Warwickshire. d 18.5.1915 Westminster, London. ed Harrow; OU (Oriel, All Souls). occ wk. Also OU (3), Oxfordshire, Warwickshire Gentlemen. President of MCC (1887). Brother of J.W. (MCC), brother-in-law of R.A.Fitzgerald, uncle of H.D.G.Leveson-Gower (England, Surrey) and F.A.G.Leveson-Gower (OU, Hampshire). Club: Maidenhead.

LEIGH, SPENCER AUSTEN (1853-60). b 17.2.1834 Speen, Newbury. d 9.12.1913 Frog Firle, Alfriston, Sussex. ed Harrow. rhb. Also Sussex. Brother of A.Austen-Leigh, A.H.Austen-Leigh, C.Austen-Leigh, C.E.Austen-Leigh, E.C.Austen-Leigh and W.Austen-Leigh. Club: Maidenhead.

LEIGH (1860).

LETTS (1853).

LILLYWHITE, FREDERICK WILLIAM (1844-46). b 13.6.1792 Westampnett, Sussex. d 21.8.1854 Islington, London. rhb. rsm. Also Sussex, Surrey, Cambridge Town, Hampshire, Middlesex. Father of F. (FC Umpire), F.H. (United States of America), John (Middlesex) and James (Middlesex and Sussex), uncle of James jun (Sussex). Professional.

MARTIN, W. (1860).

MARTINGELL, WILLIAM (1844). b 20.8.1818 Nutfield, Surrey. d 29.9.1897 Eton Wick, Buckinghamshire. rhb. rmr. Also Surrey, Kent, Hampshire, Somerset, Worcestershire, Warwickshire. Son of Russell (Surrey). Professional.

MASON, F. (1860).

MASTERS, F. (1849).

MICKLEM, HENRY (1860). b 1828 Henley-on-Thames, Oxfordshire. d 10.1.1901 Upper Culham, Henley-on-Thames, Oxfordshire. ed OU (Trinity). Brother of L.

MICKLEM, LEONARD (1870). b 12.3.1845 Henley-on-Thames, Oxfordshire. d 7.7.1919 Elstree, Hertfordshire. ed Eton; OU (Merton). rhb. Brother of H. Club: Maidenhead.

MONTAGU, Rev. GEORGE (1858). b 1.6.1820 South Pickenham, Norfolk. d 22.2.1904 Walsingham, Norfolk. ed OU (Worcester).

MORRES, ELLIOTT JAMES (1859). b 10.4.1831 Reading. d 5.11.1895 Bath, Somerset. ed Winchester; OU (Trinity). Also OU (1). Brother of H.R. and R.E., uncle of E.R and H.F.M. Club: Maidenhead.

MORRES, Rev. HUGH REDMOND (1858-60). b 1839 Wokingham. d 18.9.1882 Streatley. ed OU (Magdalene). Brother of E.J. and R.E., father of E.R. and H.F.M. Club: Maidenhead.

MORRES, Rev. ROBERT ELIOT (1858-60). b 1827 Nether Broughton, Leicestershire. d 6.4.1885 Longridge, Bath, Somerset. ed Winchester; OU (Wadham). Brother of E.J. and H.R., uncle of E.R. and H.F.M. Club: Maidenhead.

NEWTON (1857).

NICHOLSON, WILLIAM (1858). c 7.6.1820 Lincoln. d 7.4.1916 Maidenhead. Club: Maidenhead.

NORSWORTHY, GEORGE (1858-60). b 1838 London. d 5.1.1921 Bournemouth, Hampshire. ed Winchester; OU (Magdalene). Club: Maidenhead.

PAINE, HENRY (1844-57). b 7.6.1817 Shipdean, Norfolk. wk. Professional. Club: Reading.

PARRY, Captain (1846).

PAUL, EDWIN (1849). b 21.9.1822 Holloway, London. d 6.10.1858 Holloway, London. Professional. Clubs: Islington Albion, Reading, Bramshill.

PEARCE (1846).

PEARSON, Rev. ARTHUR CYRIL (1858). b 9.1.1838 Springfield, Essex. d 8.11.1916. St Leonards-on-Sea, Sussex. ed Winchester; OU (Balliol).

PERRY, WILLIAM (1849). b 12.8.1830 Oxford. d 15.3.1913 Thatcham. wk. Also Lancashire, Oxfordshire. Professional. Club: Reading.

PINNIGER, JAMES COCKBURN (1857-60). c 15.1.1830 Newbury. d 25.12.1907 Newbury.

POLLITT, JAMES PETER (1860). b 1826 St Leonard's-on-Sea, Sussex. d 4Q.1860 Brighton, Sussex. Also Middlesex, Hampshire. FC Umpire. Club: Woolwich.

PRICE, E. (1872).

PRICE, F. (1870-72).

RANDALL, Rev. JAMES LESLIE (1844). c 27.12.1828 Dorking, Surrey. d 17.1.1922 Christchurch, Hampshire. ed Winchester; OU (New).

RAYNER, Corporal (1849). Club: Horse Brigade.

READE, Rev. HENRY ST JOHN (1859-60). b 4.1.1840 Streatley. d 13.2.1884 Shepherd's Bush, Fulham, London. ed Tonbridge; OU (University). sra. wk. Also Kent, Gloucestershire, Hertfordshire, Oxfordshire.

RHODES, W. (1844-46). Club: Reading.

RICARDO, ALEXANDER LOUIS (1860). b 1843 Chelsea, London. d 19.4.1871 Cologne, Germany. Also Hampshire. Clubs: Maidenhead, Knickerbockers, Grenedier Guards.

ROBINSON, Rev. ARTHUR EDWARD (1856). b 6.12.1835 Charlton-on-Otmore, Oxfordshire. d 29.4.1884 Wootton, Oxfordshire. ed Winchester; OU (New Coll). Club: Hungerford Park.

ROGERS CHARLES (1859). b 23.3.1824 Cowley, Oxfordshire. d 23.7.1887 Cowley, Oxfordshire. Also Oxfordshire. Father of Alfred (Oxfordshire), Joseph (Oxfordshire), Henry (Oxfordshire), Peter (Oxfordshire) and William (Oxfordshire). Professional. Club: Cowley.

ROYSTON, HENRY (1849). b 12.8.1819 Harrow-on-the-Hill, Middlesex. d 30.9.1873 St John's Wood, London. rhb. rsr. Also Middlesex. Clubs: Bramshill, MCC (ground bowler).

SAMPSON, HENRY (1844). b 13.3.1813 Hallam, Sheffield, Yorkshire. d 29.3.1885 Sheffield, Yorkshire. rhb. Also Yorkshire. Father of G.H. (Otago). Professional. Club: Reading.

SIMONDS HENRY JOHN (1844). c 12.5.1828 Reading. d 25.1 1896 Caversham, Oxfordshire. ed Eton. Club: Reading.

SLADE, Rev. GEORGE FITZCLARENCE (1870). b 1832 Maunsel, Somerset. d 23.12.1904 West Buckland, Reigate, Surrey. ed Eton; OU (All Souls).

SLOCOCK, CHARLES SAMUEL (1853-59). b 1821 Donnington, Newbury. d 1.1.1907 Kensington, London. ed OU (Trinity). Father of C.E. Clubs: Reading, Maidenhead, Hungerford Park.

SLOCOCK, Rev. SAMUEL (1859). c 3.10.1832 Newbury. d 21.12.1901 Roundton, Northallerton, Yorkshire. ed Gough House, Chelsea; CU (Caius).

SMITH (1849).

SMITH, J. S. (1859). Clubs: Hungerford, Reading.

STEPHENS, CHARLES (1858). b 20.3.1831 Stonehouse, Gloucestershire. d 4.10.1901 Woodley Hill, Reading. ed Winchester; OU (Balliol). Club: Reading.

STEPHENS, Captain FREDERICK (1858-59). b 4.2.1836 Caversham Place. d 1.4.1909 Chawton, Hampshire. ed Winchester; OU (Pembroke). Also Huntingdonshire. Father of F.G.R.B. (Weigalls XI) and B.J.B. (Europeans), uncle of A.M.Byng (Hampshire).

TALBOT (1849).

WALLER, Rev. ADOLPHUS (1860). b 8.10.1839 Brussels, Belgium. d 16.7.1890 Hunstanton, Norfolk. ed Harrow; OU (Christ Church).

WALTER, Rev. HENRY MAJOR (1869). b 15.1.1850 Grosvenor Square, London. d 31.1.1931 Wokingham. ed Eton; OU (Oriel). Son of J.

WALTER, JOHN (1859). b 8.11.1818 Bearwood. d 3.11.1894 Bearwood. ed Eton; OU (Exeter). MP Nottingham (1847-59); Berkshire (1859-65, 1868-85). Father of H.M.

WEBBE, Captain GEORGE ALLAN (1872). b 15.1.1854 Westminster, London. d 19.2.1925 Ascot. ed Harrow; OU (University). rhb. Also Dorset. Brother of A.J. (England, Middlesex) and H.R. (OU, Middlesex).

WELLS, Rev. GEORGE FRANCIS (1859). b 1837 Speen. d 6.4.1916 March, Cambridgeshire. ed OU (Christ Church).

WETHERELL, F. (1859).

WILD, A. (1857).

WILDE, CHARLES ROBERT CLAUDE (1849). (Baron TRURO). b 1.11.1816 London. d 27.3.1891 Rome, Italy. ed Winchester; CU (Trinity).

WILLIAMS (1849).

WYATT (1844-46).

YONGE, GERALD EDWARD (1853-59). b 4.7.1824 Eton, Buckinghamshire. d 27.12.1904 Stoke Lodge, Bishopstoke, Hampshire. ed Eton; OU (Trinity). fr. Also OU (5), Buckinghamshire. Club: Hungerford Park.

BERKSHIRE CRICKETERS 1895-2008

AERI, VISHAL KUMAR (2006). b 20.11.1981 Ascot. rhb. rfm. Club: Reading.

ALBERTINI, WILLIAM REYNOLDS JAMES DIAZ- (1936-38). b 21.1.1913 Kensington, London. d 5.1994 Barnard, Vermont, United States of America. ed Tonbridge. Tour: Brinkman's XI to Argentina. Club: Incogniti.

ALDERMAN, ALBERT EDWARD (1950). b 30.10.1907 Alvaston, Derbyshire. d 6.6.1990 Frimley Park, Surrey. rhb. ob. Also Derbyshire (Cap). FC and MCCA Umpire. Football (Derby County, Burnley). Grandfather of T.A.J.Dawson (OU). Cricket Coach Repton College. Club: Suttons.

ALLAWAY, DAVID PHILIP JONATHAN (2006). b 6.7.1979 Reading. ed Oratory S. lhb. Club: Henley.

ALLDIS, JAMES STEPHEN (1982). b 27.12.1949 Paddington, London. lhb.sla. Also Middlesex, MCC YC. Tour: Berkshire to Hong Kong. Club: Finchley.

ALLEN, JOHN CHARLES RUSSELL (1986). b 22.2.1961 Windlesham, Surrey. rhb. rmf. Club: Royal Ascot.

ANDERSON, RICHARD GEORGE (1986). b 24.11.1961 Sonning. rhb. sla. Club: Sonning.

APPLEWHAITE, ANTHONY (1980). b 25.11.1948 Barbados. rhb. rfm. Club: Wokingham.

ARMSTRONG, JOHN DAVID G. (1971). b 1Q 1943 Surrey. Club: Hungerford.

ATKINSON, LEE DAVID (2002). b 16.7.1976 Watford, Hertfordshire. lhb. sla. Club: North Maidenhead.

ATTENBOROUGH, GEORGE MICHAEL (1969-70). b 26.8.1938 Derby. ed Rossall. rhb. sla. Club: Harrow.

AUSTIN, HENRY JAMES (1912). b 1Q.1864 Boxmoor, Hertfordshire. d 18.1.1929 Eton. Also Buckinghamshire, Hertfordshire. Professional Eton College.

AUSTIN, ROBERT JOHN (1952). b 11.11.1921 Uckfield, Sussex. ed St Edward's S, Oxford. Club: Thatcham.

BACON, BARRINGTON DAVID ('BARRY') (1958). b 26.6.1939 Oxford. ed Newbury GS; OU (St Edmund Hall). rhb. rf. Rugby (OU, Berkshire, Harlequins, English Schools). Club: Newbury.

BAILEY, WALTER GEORGE ('JOE') (1913-20). b 9.2.1890 Thame, Oxfordshire. d 20.7.1974 Weymouth, Dorset. Football (England (2, amateur), England Olympic XI, Nottingham Forest, Reading, Boscombe). Hockey (Oxfordshire).

BAINES, Canon ALFRED GEORGE PISANI (1909). b 11.1.1871 High Wycombe, Buckinghamshire. d 12.5.1949 Slough, Buckinghamshire. ed Bedford GS; OU (Keble). Also Buckinghamshire. Club: Reading.

BAINES, FREDERICK CHARLES (1963-77). b 12.11.1941 Preston, Lancashire. ed Reading S; Birmingham U. lhb. rm. Cap (1964). Also UAU. Clubs: Dunstable, Reading, Old Redingnesians, Lancaster.

BAINES, KENNETH CHARLES (1920-25). b 15.9.1898 Bradfield. d 6.1993 Ludlow, Shropshire. Rugby Union Referee. Club: Newbury.

BAKER, AIDAN FRANCIS (1996-2000). b 31.12.1964 Blackburn, Lancashire. rhb. rfm. ed St Augustines, Billington. Also Suffolk, Surrey CB. Tour: Berkshire to South Africa. Football (Bury). Club: Metropolitan Police, Weybridge.

BAKER, HENRY STUART (1910). b 3Q.1881 Wallingford. Club: Hythe.

BAKER, Major NIGEL ERNEST WESTBY (1934). b 9.1.1914 Westminster, London. d 10.3.1968 Balcombe, Sussex. ed Eton; CU (Trinity). rhb. rf. Also CU.

BAKER, PETER ANTHONY (1962-78). b 18.9.1945 Crowthorne. d 3.10.2000 Stourton, Warwickshire. ed Cheltenham. rhb. ob. wk. Also Oxfordshire (lo). Hockey (Oxfordshire). Club: Oxford Downs.

BAMPTON, ANTHONY GEORGE (1964-75). b 4.3.1942 Reading. ed Ashmead SM. rhb. Club: Reading.

BARBER, HENRY (1896). b 4Q.1865 Swallowfield, Wokingham.

BARBER, JASON (2007). b 11.3.1977 Pretoria, Transvaal, South Africa. rhb. Club: Henley.

BARKER, ALGERNON GRESLEY (1922). b 4Q.1899 Basingstoke, Hampshire. d 24.2.1924 Kuldana, India. ed Eton; RMC Sandhurst.

BARKER, WILLIAM (1895-08). b 10.3.1869 Swallowfield, Wokingham. rhb. lf. Also Surrey. MCCA Umpire. County Club Professional. Club: Reading.

BARMBY, Rev. FRANCIS JAMES (1900-09). b 24.12.1863 Pittington, Durham. d 30.9.1936 Summertown, Oxfordshire. ed Charterhouse; OU (Magdalen). rhb rm. Also OU, Durham. Football (OU).

BARNES, DAVID EDWARD (2007-08). b 27.9.1982 Whitehaven, Cumberland. ed Millom S. rhb. rm. Cap (2008). Also MCCA (u-25, lo), Cumberland, Leicestershire II, Durham II, Durham CB. Club: Reading.

BARNES, Captain JAMES DAVID KENTISH (1959). b 18.4.1930 Caldy, Wirral, Cheshire. ed Eton; RMA Sandhurst. rhb. rm. Clubs: Finchampstead, Free Foresters.

BARR, CYRIL PERCY (1936). b 25.5.1907 Wantage. d 11.10.1986 Thatcham. Club: Thatcham.

BARRETT, ARTHUR THOMAS (1970). b 24.3.1946 Chipping Norton, Oxfordshire. ed Abingdon S; Reading U. Club: Reading.

BARRETT, HARRY (1897-09). b 21.9.1873 Wokingham. rm. FC and MCCA Umpire. Clubs: Reading (pro), Berkshire Regimental Depot (pro).

BARRINGTON, Hon. PERCY EVELYN (1904). b 29.7.1884 Brackley, Northamptonshire. d 30.5.1911 Buenos Aires, Argentina. ed Charterhouse. Also Wiltshire. Brother of R.E.S. and W.B.L.

BARRINGTON, Lieut.-Colonel Hon. RUPERT EDWARD SELBORNE (1896). b 10.12.1877 Brackley, Northamptonshire. d 7.8.1975 Forest Row, Sussex. ed Charterhouse. Also Western Transvaal. Brother of P.E. and W.B.L.

BARRINGTON, Hon. WALTER BERNARD LOUIS (1895-96). b 15.5.1876 Brackley, Northamptonshire. d 12.5.1959 Hollesley, Suffolk. ed Charterhouse. Also Buckinghamshire. Brother of P.E. and R.E.S. Club: Buscot Park.

BARROW, JAMES KEITH (1990-2000). b 16.12.1964 Haslemere, Surrey. ed Churches C, Petersfield. rhb rfm. Cap (1998). Also Hampshire II. Tour: Berkshire to South Africa. Clubs: Cheam, Farnham.

BARTHOLOMEW, Major-General ARTHUR WOLLASTON (1899-1904). b 5.5.1878 Reading. d 29.1.1945 Ottery St Mary, Devon. ed Marlborough; OU (Trinity). Hockey (OU (2)). Club: Reading.

BARTLETT, HENRY ARCHIBALD DUNBAR (1921-22). b 1887 Aberdeen, Scotland. d 14.12.1968 Wokingham. Clubs: Caversham, Shepherds Bush.

BATT, CHRISTOPHER JAMES (1997-2001). b 22.9.1976 Taplow, Buckinghamshire. ed Cox Green CS. lhb. lfm. Also Sussex, Middlesex, MCCA (ST, u-25), ECB XI, Buckinghamshire, Hampshire II, Sussex II, Middlesex CB, MCC YC. Club: Reading.

BATTYE, Lieut. CYRIL WYNYARD (1914). b 3Q.1894 Wandsworth, Surrey d 13.3.1916 Netheravon, Wiltshire. ed Repton; RMC Sandhurst. Son of W. (MCC).

BEAVEN, LUKE EDWARD (2006-07). b 31.8.1989 Reading. ed Highdown S; Reading U. rhb. sla. Also MCCA (u-25), Gloucestershire II, Surrey II, MCC YC. Club: Reading.

BECKETT, Captain DONALD GEORGE (1971-75). b 2.4.1936 Singapore. d 22.8.2000 Camberley, Surrey. ed St George's C., Weybridge; RMA Woolwich. rhb. lm. Cap (1972). Also Hong Kong, Army, Combined Services. Club: Ashford (Middlesex).

BECKWITH, EDWARD ARTHUR SIDNEY MALEBYS (1934). b 31.7.1906 Stratford-upon-Avon, Warwickshire. d 5.2.1988 Penzance, Cornwall. ed Cheltenham; OU (Magdalen). Rugby (Berkshire). Squash (Berkshire). Club: Old Cheltonians.

BEDDING, ROBERT (1897-99). b 1855 Chichester, Sussex. Clubs: Reading (pro), Royal Berkshire Regiment.

BELCHER, Captain GORDON (1910-13). b 26.9.1885 Kemp Town, Brighton, Sussex. d 16.5.1915 Richebourg L'Avoune, Belgium. ed Brighton C; CU (St Catharine's). rhb.rm. Also Hampshire. Son of T.H. (OU). Club: Reading.

BELL, DAVID JOHN (1970). b 2.7.1952 Enfield, Middlesex. lhb. lmf. Also Middlesex II, Hampshire II. Club: Berkshire Bantams.

BELLAMY, L. C. S. (1950). Club: Maidenhead and Bray.

BENNETT, Major GEORGE GUY MARSLAND (1902-27). b 22.4.1883 Didsbury, Manchester, Lancashire. d 6.2.1966 Sunningdale. ed Harrow; OU (Magdalene). rhb. rfm. Also OU, MCCA (sc), Lancashire II. Brother of J.H.

BENNETT, JOHN HADFIELD (1906-08). b 11.8.1885 Didsbury, Manchester, Lancashire. d 27.5.1973 Littleham, Exmouth, Devon. ed Harrow; OU (Magdalen). Hockey (England (Captain 1921-24), OU (2), Berkshire). Brother of G.G.M.

BERRY, FRED (1947-50). b 13.2.1910 Kirkheaton, Yorkshire. d 2.1.1989 Bracknell. rhb. rmf. Cap (1947). Also Surrey, MCCA (fc). MCCA Umpire. Coach Wellington College.

BETTS, JOHN EDWARD ARNOTT (1925). b 29.04.1900 Kings Langley, Hertfordshire. d 10.11.1990 Oxford. ed Imperial Service C; Reading U. Club: Old Berkhampstead.

BIRCH, HUGH HAMILTON CRAIG (1922). b 4Q.1892 Feltham, Middlesex. d 3.12.1977 Tokers Green, Reading. Club: Reading.

BLOOMFIELD, TIMOTHY FRANCIS (1996). b 31.5.1973 Ashford, Middlesex. ed Halliford S. rhb. rfm. Also Middlesex (Cap 2001), Sussex II. Tours: MCC to Sri Lanka; to Kenya. Clubs: Finchampstead, Staines.

BLOYCE, STEPHEN MICHAEL (2003-04). b 11.11.1980 Crowthorne. ed Edgbarrow S; Farnborough C; Chelsea S, Brighton. rhb. rfm. Also Essex II. Club: Finchampstead.

BLUNDELL, Captain DERMOT HOWARD BLUNDELL-HOLLINSHEAD- (1895-04). b 27.2.1874 Westminster, London. d 26.10.1910 Kensington, London. ed Wellington. rhb. Also MCC. Brother-in-law of G.E.F.Ward (MCC). Club: Kings Royal Rifles.

BOMFORD, Flying Officer CHARLES POWELL (1938). b 5.5.1915 Robinstown, Meath, Ireland. d 9.6.1940 Dieppe, France. ed Wickham House; Eastbourne C. Cap (1938).

BORGNIS, RICHARD PETER (later HAMMOND-CHAMBERS-BORGNIS) (1931). 25.8.1910 Newbury. d 28.5.2001 Payron, France. rhb. rm. Also Combined Services, Royal Navy. Nephew of H.D.G.Leveson-Gower (England, Surrey, OU).

BOYCE (1911).

BRADBURN, PETER NORMAN (1979-83). b 27.3.1954 Hammersmith, London. ed Repton; Birmingham U. rhb.lm. Also UAU. Clubs: Repton Pilgrims, Redditch.

BRADBURY, PETER CHARLES (1974). b 29.9.1946 Edgware, Middlesex. rhb. Club: Finchampstead.

BRADFIELD, G. R. (1910).

BRADFIELD, SIDNEY ROBERT (1935-37). b 4Q.1909 Reading. Groundsman Reading CC. Club: Suttons.

BRADFIELD, THOMAS (1903). b 4Q.1873 Shinfield, Wokingham. Club: Swallowfield.

BRADLEY, ROBERT HENRY (1939). b 30.5.1922 Reading. ed Lancing C. Club: Lancing College.

BRAMWELL-DAVIS, Major-General ROBERT ALBERT (1933). b 8.10.1905. d 12.5.1974 Downton, Salisbury, Wiltshire. ed Wellington; RMC Sandhurst. Club: Berkshire Gentlemen.

BROCKLEHURST, BENJAMIN GILBERT (1955). b 18.2.1922 Knapton, Norfolk. d 17.6.2007. Tunbridge Wells, Kent. ed Bradfield. rhb. Also Somerset (Captain 1953-54, Cap 1953). Father-in-law of R.A.Hutton, grandfather of B.L.Hutton (Middlesex) and O.R.Hutton (OUCCE). Clubs: Finchampstead, Bradfield Waifs.

BROCKWAY, WALTER CHARLES (1946). b 7.3.1907 Blandford Forum, Dorset. d 15.6.1985 Harare, Zimbabwe. lhb. sla. Also Hampshire, Eastern Province, Dorset. Club: Reading (pro).

BRODIE, JAMES BRUCE (1960). b 19.3.1937 Graaf-Reinet, Cape Province, South Africa. ed Union HS, South Africa; CU (Fitzwilliam). rhb. rfm. Cap (1960). Also CU (1), Eastern Province. Club: Etceteras

BROGAN, STEPHEN MICHAEL (2002-03). b 24.9.1969 Worksop, Nottinghamshire. ed Manor CS, Mansfield; Sheffield P. rhb. Also Herefordshire, Nottinghamshire CB, Derbyshire II, Nottinghamshire II. Club: Finchampstead.

BROOKS, CHARLES EDWARD WILLIAM (1951-66). b 17.2.1927. Epsom, Surrey. d 18.5.2002 Abingdon. rhb. lb. Cap (1955). Also Surrey II. Clubs: Oxford City, Abingdon, Berkshire Gentlemen.

BROOKS, RICHARD ALAN (1977). b 14.6.1943 Edgware, Middlesex. ed Quinton; Bristol U; OU (St Edmund Hall). rhb. wk. Also OU (1), Somerset (Cap 1968). Club: Bradfield Waifs.

BROUGHAM, Major HENRY (1905-13). b 8.7.1888 Wellington College, Crowthorne. d 18.2.1923 La Croix, Var, France. rhb. ed Wellington; OU (Brasenose). Also OU (1), MCCA (fc), Public Schools. Racquets (OU), Rugby (England (4), Harlequins). Brother-in-law of J.H.Bruce-Lockhart, uncle of RB Bruce-Lockhart (CU).

BROW, ANDREW DOUGLAS BROMFIELD (1956-57). b 28.2.1933 Reading. ed Aldenham. lhb. sla. Clubs: Mapledurham, Berkshire Gentlemen.

BROWN, CHARLES EDWARD (1900-05). b 1Q.1855 Hereford. Also Herefordshire. FC and MCCA Umpire. Professional Bradfield College.

BROWN, Rev. LIONEL GEORGE (1901). b 23.4.1872 Ancaster, Lincolnshire. d 16.12.1938 Chapel, Chorlton, Staffordshire. ed Bedford Modern S; OU (Merton). rhb. wk. Also OU, Bedfordshire. Billiards (OU (Blue)). Club: Reading.

BROWN, ROBERT ROSS BUCHANAN (1938-39). b 15.7.1909 Sydney, New South Wales, Australia. d 7.9.2001 Wargrave. ed King's S, Sydney; Sydney U; CU (Emmanuel).

BROWNE, Rev. FRANCIS DESHON (1907). b 1871 Cananore, India. d 10.2.1940 Wokingham. ed Newton C.; CU (Jesus). rhb. Father-in-law of G.F.Cameron. Club: Maidenhead.

BROWNING, GEOFFREY ALEXANDER (1929). b 21.3.1909 South Africa. d 12.8.1939 Chelsea, London. ed Eton; OU (Worcester). Club: Worcester College.

BUCKHAM, ARTHUR HAROLD (1939). b 19.3.1916. Reigate, Surrey. d 14.3.1996 Winchester, Hampshire. ed Bradfield.

BUCKLEY, CYRIL FRANCIS STEWART (1924-35). b 21.2.1905 Chelsea, London. d 11.6.1974 Chelsea, London. ed Eton. wk. Also Leveson-Gower's XI. Great-nephew of A. (MCC) and D.F. (MCC).

BUNCE, JOHN MALCOLM (1962-69). b 27.1.1944 Oxford, Oxfordshire. ed Abingdon S; Loughborough C. lhb. ob. Club: Abingdon.

BURGESS, LEWIS ALBERT (otherwise Albert Lewis) (1895-96). b 2Q. 1874 Sutton Scotney, Hampshire. d 24.4.1949 Reading. Club: Reading Biscuit Factory.

BURGOYNE, WILLIAM ARTHUR (1975-76). b 28.10.1942 Windsor. rhb. rmf. Cap (1975). Club: Streatham.

BURROW, STEPHEN (1980-83). b 13.1.1958 Wokingham. ed Emmbrook S, Reading. rhb. rm. Cap (1980). Also MCCA, Buckinghamshire (Cap 1985), Hertfordshire, Middlesex II, Surrey II, Hampshire II, MCC YC. Club: North Middlesex.

BURROWS, THOMAS GEORGE (2001-03). b 5.5.1985 Reading. ed Reading S. rhb. wk. Also Hampshire. Tour: MCC to Namibia and Uganda. Club: Finchampstead.

CAME, Brigadier KENNETH CHARLES (1956-57). b 29.10.1925 Caversham. d 29.1.1986 Up Nately, Basingstoke, Hampshire. ed Bournemouth S. lhb. rm. Also Army. Father of P.R.C. (Hampshire II), son-in-law of R.W.V. Robins (England, Middlesex), brother-in-law of R.V.C. Robins (Middlesex). Clubs: Bradfield Waifs, Free Foresters.

CAMERON, GUY FREMANTLE (1924-25). b 11.1894 St Lucia, West Indies. d 13.12.1956 Bradford Abbas, Sherborne, Dorset. ed Uppingham; OU (Brasennose). Son-in-law of F.D. Browne. Club: Berkshire Amateurs.

CARE, PERCY MARTIN (1926). b 25.9.1893 Tottenham, London. d 7.9.1990 Newquay, Cornwall. Club: Wargrave.

CARLESS, Dr. JEREMY JOHN (1957). b 4.4.1938 Hong Kong. ed Charterhouse; St Mary's Hospital, London U. rhb. rm. Also Public Schools, Tennis (Public Schools Doubles Champions). Brother of R.P. (Combined Services). Club: Charterhouse Friars.

CARR, Captain JOHN LILLINGSTON (1926-36). b 16.5.1892 Palamcottah, India. d 3.2.1963 Derby. ed Repton; St Lawrence C, Ramsgate; OU (Magdalen). Also Army. Football (OU (1)). Hockey (Berkshire, Army). Father of D.B. (Derbyshire) and D.J. (Free Foresters), grandfather of J.D. (Middlesex). Clubs: Berkshire Amateurs, Royal Berkshire Regiment.

CARTER, Captain (RN) NORMAN HUNTER (1901). b 3Q.1877 Mortimer. d 4Q.1949 Netherbury, Bridport, Dorset. ed RNC Britannia.

CARTER, PAUL RICHARD (2001-08). b 14.5.1982 Reading. ed Gillott's S, Henley; Cox Green CS; Loughborough U. rhb. ob. Cap (2008). Also MCCA (ST, u-25), British Universities, Gloucestershire II, Worcestershire II. Clubs: Finchampstead, Henley.

CARTMELL, NEIL DAVID JOHN (1991-94). b 15.7.1968 Harrow, Middlesex. ed St Dominic SFC. rhb. wk. Also Nottinghamshire II, Middlesex II, Derbyshire II. Club: Maidenhead and Bray.

CARYER, REGINALD GEORGE (1928-35). b 28.9.1895 West Hougham, Dover, Kent. d 7.6.1957 Reading. rhb. rmf. Also Sussex. Groundsman Reading CC. Club: Huntley and Palmers.

CASEMORE, COLIN (1970-77). b 21.2.1940 St Mellons, Monmouthshire. ed Hove GS; Imperial C. London U. rhb. lb. Cap (1971). Also Sussex II, ESCA. Football (British Universities, Sussex). Clubs: Maidenhead and Bray, Bushey.

CASLON, CHRISTIAN ANDRIES (1929). b 17.1.1893. d 23.8.1955 Marylebone, London. ed Highgate. Also Public Schools.

CASTELL, ALAN RICHARD (1971-73). b 4Q 1940 Basingstoke, Hampshire. rhb. Cap (1972). Also Hampshire II. Club: Reading.

CAUDLE, JOHN (1938-39). b 20.11.1920 Banbury, Oxfordshire. d 7.5.1991 Uffculme, Devon. ed Reading S. Club: Reading.

CAVE, ALAN DARLINGTON (1926). b 19.12.1904 Ware, Hertfordshire. d 6.12.1983 Wokingham. ed Rugby; OU (Trinity). Golf (Britain, OU (Blue)). Brother of J.D. Club: Maidenhead and Bray.

CAVE, JOHN DARLINGTON (1925-26). b 1.2.1898 Ware, Hertfordshire. d 17.11.1981 Bristol, Gloucestershire. ed Rugby; OU (Balliol). Golf (OU (Blue)). Brother of A.D. Club: Maidenhead and Bray.

CAVE, WILLIAM (1899-1911). b 4.8.1867 Newbury. d 25.3.1938 Newbury. Also Hampshire. Club: Newbury (pro).

CAWSTON, EDWARD (1937-46). b 16.1.1911 Wantage. d 5.9.1998 Maidstone, Kent. ed Lancing; CU (Pembroke). rhb. rm. Cap (1938). Also Sussex, CU (1), Suffolk, RAF, Egypt. Tours: Martineau to Egypt (2). Athletics (CU (Blue)).

CHALONER, WILLIAM HUGH (2006). b 4.12.1986 Reading. rhb. ob. Club: Falkland.

CHAMBERLAIN, TIMOTHY PHILIP VENTRESS (2006). b 15.1.1983 Oxford. rhb. rfm. Club: Henley.

CHANCE, Major GEOFFREY HENRY BARRINGTON (1912-13). b 16.12.1893 Burghfield. d 11.7.1987 Braydon Hall, Minety, Wiltshire. ed Eton. lhb. rm. Also Hampshire.

CHAPMAN, ARTHUR PERCY FRANK (1920-24). b 3.9.1900 The Mount, Reading. d 16.9.1961 Alton, Hampshire. ed Uppingham; Oakham; CU (Pembroke). lhb. sla. Also England (26, Captain (17)), CU (3), Kent (Captain 1931-36, Cap 1925), MCCA. Tours: MCC to Australia and New Zealand; to Australia (2); to South Africa; Tennyson to Jamaica; Martineau to Egypt. Son of F.E., nephew of C.E., C.E.Finch and F.W.Finch, brother-in-law of T.C.Lowry (New Zealand, Somerset). Club: Wokingham.

CHAPMAN, Rev. CHARLES EDWARD (1895). b 26.8.1860 Swinstead, Lincolnshire. d 23.8.1901 Scrivelsby, Lincolnshire. ed Horncastle GS; Trent C; CU (Sidney Sussex). rhb. rf. Also CU, Lincolnshire, Hampshire Gentlemen. Rugby (England (1), CU). Brother of F.E., brother-in-law of F.W.Finch, uncle of A.P.F. Club: Reading.

CHAPMAN, FRANK EMERSON (1895-1900). b 2Q.1863 Horncastle, Lincolnshire. d 27.11.1941 Wokingham. ed Oakham; CU (Sidney Sussex). wk. Father of A.P.F., brother of C.E., brother-in-law of F.W.Finch. Club: Reading.

CHEESEMAN, BRIAN ELDON FREDERICK (1963-66). b 14.6.1929 Shefford Woodlands. ed Marlborough. rhb. ob. Also Surrey II. Rugby (Blackheath). Club: Maidenhead and Bray.

CHILD, DAVID (1971). b 23.9.1941 Newbury. rhb.

CHILD, GORDON EDWARD JAMES (1967-85). b 7.11.1939 The Mumbles, Glamorgan. ed Cathays GS; Cardiff U. rhb. wk. County Club Captain (1979-81). Cap (1967). Also Glamorgan II. Tours: Berkshire to Hong Kong; to South Africa (Manager). Clubs: Maidenhead and Bray, Reading.

CHRISTOPHERSON, PERCY (1897-98). b 31.3.1866 Kidbrooke, Blackheath, Kent. d 4.5.1921 Folkestone, Kent. ed Bedford GS; Marlborough; OU (University). rhb. rf. Also OU, Kent. Rugby (England (2), OU(3), Blackheath). Brother of S. (Kent), uncle of S.Akers-Douglas (OU, Kent). Club: Blackheath.

CLARKE, CHARLES FREDERICK CARLOS (1896). b 26.4.1853 Welton, Northamptonshire. d 29.1.1931 Virginia Water, Surrey. rhb. sra. Also Surrey. Brother of M.C. (Surrey), father-in-law of N.C.Tufnell (Surrey). Club: Silwood Park.

CLARKE, GLEN (1974). b 25.5.1948 Barbados. rhb. rm. Also Kent II. Club: Bracknell.

CLAUGHTON, JOHN ALAN (1982-85). b 17.9.1956 Guiseley, Yorkshire. ed KES, Birmingham; OU (Merton). rhb. sla. Cap (1983). Also Warwickshire, OU (4, Captain 1978), MCCA (BHC), Dorset. Great-nephew of H.M. (Yorkshire), nephew of J.A. (OU). Coach Bradfield School. Club: Richmond.

COBHAM, MICHAEL DAVID (1948). b 11.5.1930 Boynton, Yorkshire. ed Stowe. rhb. rmf. Club: Stowe School.

COLGATE, Dr. REGINALD THOMAS (1929). b 31.3.1889 Newhaven, Sussex. d 27.3.1970 Twyford. ed City and Guilds C.; London U. Club: Reading Biscuit Factory.

COLLINS, ANDREW JAMES (1997). b 24.7.1972 Andover, Hampshire. d 25.2.1999 London. ed Cricklade C; Cheltenham and Gloucester CHE. rhb. rm. Also Herefordshire, Wiltshire, Hampshire II, Gloucestershire II. Club: Falkland.

COLLINS, Commander (RN) CHARLES JAMES (1902-05). b 22.11.1869 Reading. d 12.8.1908 Folkestone, Kent. ed Dover Preparatory S.

COLLINS, LEOPOLD GEORGE ARTHUR (1895-1901). b 18.6.1871 Reading. d 21.7.1947 Folkestone, Kent. ed Marlborough. Brother of L.P. and R.J. Club: Reading.

COLLINS, Brigadier LIONEL PETER (1897-1913). b 27.11.1878 Reading. d 28.9.1957 Fleet, Hampshire. ed Marlborough; OU (Keble). rhb. Also OU (1), Army and Navy, Punjab. Tour: MCC to North America. Hockey (OU (3), Berkshire). Brother of L.G.A. and R.J., father-in-law of L.E.Hunt (CU), brother-in-law of S.R.Oliver (Hampshire). Club: Reading.

COLLINS, Major General ROBERT JOHN (1908-09). b 22.8.1880 Reading. d 6.3.1950 Winchester, Hampshire. ed Marlborough. Brother of L.G.A. and L.P. Club: Wargrave.

COLLMANN, HERBERT LEONARD (1899-00). b 4Q.1875 Hulme, Manchester, Lancashire. d 23.2.1930 Hampton-on-Thames, Middlesex. Club: Windsor Home Park.

COOK, Dr. GEOFFREY WILLIAM (1967-70). b 9.2.1936 Beckenham, Kent. ed Dulwich; CU (Queen's). rhb. ob. Also Kent, CU (2), Public Schools. Tour: MCC to East Africa. Club: Datchet.

COOKE, OCTAVIUS TINSLEY (1897). b 1Q.1858 Wargrave. d 23.5.1927 Colchester, Essex. ed Felsted; CU (Jesus). Football (Upton Park).

CORRY, Dr. HARRY BARRETT (1899). b 2Q.1880 East Dulwich, Surrey. d 15.2.1965 Haslemere, Surrey. ed Reading S; CU (Caius); London Hospital. Athletics (OU (Blue)). Also Middlesex II. Club: Reading School.

COTTON, CHARLES KENNETH (1912). b 4Q.1887 Sonning. ed Tonbridge; CU (Downing).

COTTRELL, HAROLD COCHRANE (1930-33). b 24.8.1907 Reading. d 10.1987 Reading. Club: Reading.

COUZENS, MERVYN (1972). b 26.6.1936 Kintbury. rhb. rmf. Club: Newbury.

COX, CLIVE LANSBURY FIENNES (1948). b 20.1.1912 Andover, Hampshire. d 11.6.1979 Basingstoke, Hampshire. ed Wellingborough. Also Western Command. Club: Richmond.

CRESSWELL, HUGH FRANKHAM (1930). b 15.9.1908 Reading. d 2.1994 Exeter, Devon. Rugby (Berkshire, Berkshire Wanderers).

CRICHTON, HENRY THOMPSON (1913). b 18.5.1884 Edgbaston, Warwickshire. d 1.7.1968 Branksome Park, Poole, Dorset. ed KES, Birmingham. rhb. rm. Also Warwickshire. Great-grandfather of J.O.Troughton (Warwickshire).

CRISFIELD, CYRIL RAYMOND (1937-48). b 3.10.1908 Kingston upon Thames, Surrey. d 2.1988 Reading. Clubs: Reading, Thames Ditton.

CROMBIE, COLIN MALCOLM STUART (1952-58). b 26.12.1932 Newbury. d 9.6.2008 Reading. ed Reading S. lhb. ra. Cap (1956). County Club Honorary Secretary (1990-94). Club: Reading.

CROOK, HENRY SUTCLIFFE (1903). b 20.9.1874 Kidderminster, Worcestershire. ed Hereford Cathedral S; CU (Selwyn). Club: Reading.

CROOM, Corporal ALFRED BRINE (1897-1920). b 1Q.1873 St Pancras, London. Father of A.J.W., grandfather of L.C.B. (Warwickshire). Professional Reading School. Club: Reading (pro).

CROOM, ALFRED JOHN WILLIAM (1914-22). b 23.5.1896 Reading. d 16.8.1947 Oldbury, Worcestershire. rhb. ob. Also Warwickshire. Son of A.B., father of L.C.B. (Warwickshire). Club: Reading Biscuit Factory.

CROOME, ARTHUR CAPEL MOLYNEUX (1895-1905). b 21.2.1866 Stroud, Gloucestershire. d 11.9.1930 Taplow, Buckinghamshire. ed Wellington; OU (Magdalen). rhb. sra. County Club Captain (1896-99). Also Gloucestershire, OU (2). Father of Victor (RAF). Club: Reading.

CROWE, CARL DANIEL (2003-08). b 25.11.1975 Leicester. ed Lutterworth GS. rhb. ob. Cap (2005). Also Leicestershire, Leicestershire CB, NAYC. Brother of C.P. Club: Leicester Ivanhoe.

CROWE, CRAIG PIERS (2007-08). b 18.11.1979 Leicester. ed Lutterworth GS. rhb. rm. Cap (2008). Also Leicestershire II, Somerset II, Derbyshire II, Sussex II, Nottinghamshire II, Essex II, Leicestershire CB. Brother of C.D. Club: Leicester Ivanhoe.

CRUTTENDEN, ROGER (1979). b 5.10.1944 Hastings, Sussex. rhb. rfm. Also Kent II, British Police. Club: Holmesdale (Kent).

CRYER, DENNIS WILLIAM (1967-74). b 20.8.1945 Lancaster, Lancashire. ed Reading S. rhb. ob. Clubs: Newbury, Hungerford.

CUTHBERTSON, ARTHUR WILLIAM (1946-54). b 7.2.1927 Letchworth, Hertfordshire. ed Westbury GS. lhb. lm. Son of A. (MCC, Hertfordshire). Club: Reading.

DAFFEN, ARTHUR (1896-97). b 30.12.1861 Retford, Nottinghamshire. d 9.7.1938 Victoria Park, Perth, Western Australia, Australia. rhb. rf. Also Kent (Cap 1890). Club: Grange.

DAFT, RICHARD PARR (1896). b 25.10.1863 Radcliffe on Trent, Nottinghamshire. d 27.3.1934 South Croydon, Surrey. ed Trent C. rhb. rm. Also Nottinghamshire. Son of R. (Nottinghamshire), brother of H.B. (Nottinghamshire), nephew of C.F. (Nottinghamshire). Club: Notts Castle.

DANDO, MAURICE (1906). b 2Q.1886 Wells, Somerset. Club: Wallingford.

DARKIN, BERTRAM DUNCAN (1906). b 15.7.1882 Croydon, Surrey. d 1Q.1966 Croydon, Surrey. Club: Reading.

DAUGLISH, MAURICE JOHN (1896-99). b 2.10.1867 St Pancras, London. d 30.4.1922 Hunton Bridge, Hertfordshire. ed Harrow; OU (Magdalen). rhb. lob. wk. Also Middlesex, OU (2).

DAVID, Lieut.-Colonel MARKHAM (1910). b 16.1.1877 Dacca, India. d 29.9.1941 Monmouth. ed Cheltenham; CU (Clare). Also Monmouthshire.

DAVIDGE, PAUL MICHAEL (2003). b 5.1.1982 Harlow, Essex. rhb. wk. Also Bedfordshire, Huntingdonshire, Wiltshire. Club: Finchampstead.

DAVIES, RICHARD JOHN (1979). b 11.2.1954 Selly Oak, Warwickshire. ed Westlake HS, Auckland, New Zealand; Marple Hall GS. rhb. rm. Also Warwickshire, Army, Combined Services. Cricket Coach Lancing College. Club: British Police.

DAVIS, ANDREW CLIFFORD JOHN (1998). b 22.5.1964 St John's Wood, London. ed Salvatorian C; St Dominic's SFC, Harrow; Hatfield P. rhb. wk. Club: Reading.

DAVIS, ANTHONY TILTON (1950-74) b 14.8.1931 Reading. d 20.11.1978 Reading. ed Reading S; CU (St John's). rhb. sla. County Club Captain (1960-70). Cap (1954). Also MCCA. Club: Reading.

DAVIS, CHRISTOPHER JOHN DUSSER (1959). b 6.1941 Surrey. ed Bradfield; OU (Christ Church). Clubs: Bradfield Waifs, Weybridge.

DAVIS, EDWARD THOMAS W. (1901-04). b 1Q.1878 Wallingford. Club: Wallingford.

DAVIS, RICHARD PETER (2001). b 18.3.1966 Westbrook, Margate, Kent. d 29.12.2003 Blean, Kent. ed King Ethelbert's S, Birchington; Thanet TC. rhb. sla. Also Kent (Cap 1990), Leicestershire, Warwickshire (Cap 1994), Gloucestershire, Sussex, Derbyshire II, NAYC. Tour: Warwickshire to Zimbabwe. Brother-in-law of R.Sharma (Kent).

DAY, ALAN RICHARD (1977-80). b 12.11.1938 Muswell Hill, Middlesex. ed Aldenham. rhb. Cap (1978). Also Hertfordshire, Middlesex II, MCC, Free Foresters. Club: North Oxford.

DE VITRE, Captain EDWARD CHRISTOPHER DENIS (1920-28). b 3Q.1898 Wantage. d 10.1.1941 Loxwood, Billinghurst, Sussex. ed Sherborne. Also Malaya. Club: Berkshire Gentlemen.

DE VRIES, MYLES FALLOWS (1958). b 1940. ed Wellington. Also Coast CA, Kenya. Club: Bracknell.

DEDMAN, RICHARD THOMAS (1931-49). b 3.12.1908 Wandsworth, Surrey. d 3Q.1976 Shepway, Kent. rhb. ob. Cap (1939). Also British Police.

DELME-RADCLIFFE, ARTHUR HENRY (1897). b 23.11.1870 South Tidworth, Hampshire. d 30.6.1950 Branksome Park, Dorset. ed Sherborne; OU (Exeter). rhb. rs. Also Hampshire. Club: Elwood Park.

DEMPSEY, General Sir MILES CHRISTOPHER (1926-32). b 15.12.1896 Wallasey, Cheshire. d 5.6.1969 Yattenden, Newbury. ed Shrewsbury; RMC Sandhurst. rhb. sla. Also Sussex.

DENNESS, ANTHONY CHARLES (1961-71). b 23.9.1936 Hampton, Middlesex. d 15.5.2008 Grainville, France. rhb. rfm. Cap (1963). Clubs: Reading, Maidenhead and Bray.

DENNING, JOHN EDEN DE WINTON (1912-13). b 1Q.1888 Bridgewater, Somerset. d 28.1.1954 Thames Ditton, Surrey. ed Hurstpierpoint. Football (Middlesex). Club: Ealing.

DENNING, NICHOLAS ALEXANDER (2000-08). b 3.10.1978 Ascot. ed Cheltenham; Bradfield. rhb. rfm. Cap (2002). Also MCCA (ST, lo), Essex, Northamptonshire II, Surrey II, MCC YC. Club: Finchampstead.

DIGBY, JAMES R. (1955). b 3Q.1936 Sleaford, Lincolnshire. ed Reading S. Club: Reading.

DINDAR, ANDREW (1981-84). b 26.6.1942 Johannesburg, Transvaal, South Africa. rhb. rm. occ. wk. Cap (1981). Also Gloucestershire, Hertfordshire, Hampshire II, Middlesex II. Tour: Berkshire to Hong Kong. Coach Reading School. Club: Reading (pro).

DIXON, W. HOWARD (1895). Club: Bracknell.

DODD, TIMOTHY PATRICK JOHNSTONE (1987-96). b 21.4.1961 Hammersmith, London. ed Aldenham S; Loughborough U. rhb. rm. Cap (1988). Also Middlesex II, Surrey II, Somerset II, Sussex II. Tours: Berkshire to New Zealand; to South Africa. Clubs: Reading, Horsham.

DOE, LEONARD MONTAGUE (1924). b 2Q. 1894 Reading.

DOLLERY, HORACE EDGAR ('TOM') (1930-33). b 14.10.1914 Reading. d 20.1.1987 Edgbaston, Warwickshire. ed Reading S. rhb. wk. Also England (4), Warwickshire (Captain 1949-55), Wellington (New Zealand), MCCA (fc). Tour: MCC to India (tour cancelled because of War). Football (Reading). Clubs: Reading School, Moseley.

DOUGLAS, Rev. JAMES SHOLTO (1929-30). b 28.2.1892 Sherborne, Dorset. d 2.2.1974 Lingfield, Surrey. ed St Edward's S, Oxford; Wells TC. rhb. rf. Club: Pangbourne Nautical College.

DOWELL, JOHN HADLEY (1896-05). b 3Q.1869 Ryton-on-Dunsmore, Warwickshire. d 13.3.1951 Reading. Club: Reading Biscuit Factory.

DOWSE, BENJAMIN LANGFORD RICHARD (1935). b 28.11.1906 Wandsworth, Surrey. d 7.8.1983 Reading. ed Reading S. Club: Old Redingensians.

DREW, REGINALD G. (1953-54). rhb. rm. Cap (1953). Club: Wallingford

DREWETT, JOHN S. (1961-65). b 4Q.1932 Windsor. ed Reading U. wk. Cap (1963). Rugby (Berkshire, Richmond). Club: Windsor and Eton.

DUNLOP, BRUCE ELLICE (1939). b 2Q.1921 Chelsea, London. d 17.4.1943 Medjez-el-Bab, Tunisia. ed Charterhouse. Club: Charterhouse School.

DYMENT, ROBIN ERIC ADRIAN (1957-61). b 26.9.1932 Reading. rhb. wk. Cap (1958). Club: Reading.

EADES, GEORGE (1895). b 30.10.1870 Sunninghill. lf. County Club Professional.

EASBY, THOMAS JOHN (1946-53). b 15.2.1925 Henley-on-Thames, Oxfordshire. ed Reading S; OU (Jesus). rhb. rm. Club: Old Redingensians.

EDWARDS, Lieut.-Colonel CHARLES MACKENZIE (1895). b 1859 Mozuffurnygar, India. d 8.5.1936 Froyle, Alton, Hampshire.

EDWARDS, GARETH IAN (1997-01). b 30.11.1973 Exeter, Devon. ed Clyst Vale Community C; Exeter SFC; Cheltenham and Gloucester CHE. rhb. rfm. Also MCCA (u-25). Club: Reading.

EDWARDS, HORACE WALTER (1900-04). b 2Q. 1866 Maidenhead. wk. Club: Maidenhead (pro).

ELGOOD, Brigadier BERNARD CYRIL (1949). b 10.3.1922 Hampstead, London. d 10.7.1997 Pauntley Place, Redmarley, Gloucestershire. ed Bradfield; CU (Pembroke). rhb. occ. wk. Also CU (1), Combined Services, Army. Squash (CU (Blue)). Fives (CU (Blue)). Brother of R.L. Club: Bradfield Waifs.

ELGOOD, RONALD LLOYD (1949). b 8.1925 Battle, Sussex. ed Bradfield; CU (St John's). Squash (Berkshire, CU (Blue)). Fives (CU (Blue)). Brother of B.C. Club: Bradfield Waifs.

ELLISON, CHRISTOPHER JOHN (2004-05). b 12.4.1979 Sheffield, Yorkshire. ed Penrice S.; Austell C.; Exeter U. rhb. sla. Also Cornwall, Yorkshire II, Somerset II, Sussex II, Durham CB, NAYC. Brother of S.J. (Cornwall). Club: Henley.

ELPHICK, CHARLES DOUGLAS (1899-00). b 1Q.1873 Lewes, Suffolk. d 12.4.1941 Althorpe, South Africa. Coach Radley College. Professional.

EMBUREY, JOHN ERNEST (2000). b 20.8.1952 Peckham, London. ed Manor SS, Peckham. rhb. ob. Also England (64), Middlesex (Cap 1977), Northamptonshire, Western Province. Tours: England to Australia (4); to India (3); to West Indies (2); to Sri Lanka (1); to Sharjah (1); to Pakistan (1); to New Zealand (1). Robins to Sri Lanka. Middlesex to Zimbabawe. England XI to South Africa (2). Club: Maidenhead and Bray.

ENGLAND, RICHARD MICHAEL (1936-39). b 23.8.1918 Midgham, Newbury. d 10.2007 Woolhampton, Reading. ed Eton; OU (Magdalen). rhb. wk. Also OU. Club: Eton Ramblers.

ENGLISH, CHRISTOPHER BARRINGTON MARK (1978). b 12.6.1947 Bromley, Kent. ed Sir Roger Manwood's S., Sandwich. lhb. sla. Also Zambia. Club: Sonning.

ETTRIDGE, JAMES WILLIAM (2003). b 28.7.1971 Keynsham, Somerset. rhb. Club: Thatcham.

EVANS, ROBERT GORDON (1935-36). b 20.8.1899 Great Barton, Suffolk. d 2.8.1981 Sidlesham, Sussex. ed King Edward S, Bury St Edmunds; CU (Peterhouse). lhb. rfm. Also CU (1). Club: Free Foresters.

EVANS, ROBERT JOHN MARTIN (1973-74). b 14.9.1945 Farnham, Buckinghamshire. ed Abingdon S. rhb. wk. Club: Finchampstead.

FERNIE, ARTHUR ERNEST (1907). b 9.4.1877 Stone, Staffordshire. d 24.7.1959 Bideford, Devon. ed Wellingborough; CU (Clare). rhb. sla. Also CU (2), Staffordshire. Brother of A.F. (Staffordshire) and J.F. (Staffordshire).

FERRYMAN, Lieut. HUGH MOCKLER- (1909-14). b 3.5.1892 Maidstone, Kent. d 16.9.1914 Soupir, Aisne, France. ed Wellington.

FIELD, EDWIN (1895). b 18.12.1871 Hampstead, London. d 9.1.1947 South Bromley, Middlesex. ed Clifton; CU (Trinity). rhb. rm. Also Middlesex, CU (1). Rugby (England (2), CU (Blue), Middlesex W). Club: Sonning.

FINCH, FRANCIS WALTER (1895-01). b 6.1867 Wokingham. d 26.7.1936 Wokingham. ed Haileybury. rs. Uncle of A.P.F.Chapman, brother-in-law of F.E.Chapman and C.E.Chapman. Clubs: Reading, Wokingham.

FINCH, ROBERT A. (1956-62) ed Reading U. rhb. ra. Club: Woodley.

FITZHUGH, GARRY JEFFREY (1971-73). b 17.2.1942 Rugby, Warwickshire. rhb. Club: Wallingford.

FITZSIMONS, JOHN HENRY (PETER) (1960-62). b 1Q.1943 Abingdon. ed Salesian C, Oxford. Athletics (Commonwealth Games Javelin (Gold (1966), Bronze (1970)). Club: Reading.

FLATMAN, ARTHUR WILLIAM (1950-58). b 3.7.1921 Reading. d 9.12.1989 Reading. ed Reading S. sla. Cap. Club: Huntley and Palmers.

FLOWER, JOHN ERNEST (1964-70). b 7.11.1938 Chislehurst, Kent. ed Sidcup S; St Andrews U. rhb. rmf. Cap (1968). Also Norfolk. Club: Reading.

FORD, JOHN RICHARD (1955-63). b 21.8.1930. d 28.11.2003 Dalston, Carlisle, Cumberland. rhb. rm. Cap (1961). Also Cumberland. Club: Reading.

FORTIN, RICHARD CHALMERS GORDON (1965-70). b 12.4.1941 Singapore. ed Wellington; OU (Corpus Christi). rhb wk. Cap (1965). Also OU, Middlesex II. Nephew of D.J.W.Bridge (Dorset, OU). Club: Free Foresters.

FOSTER, DAREN JOSEPH (1994-95). 14.3.1966 Tottenham, Middlesex. ed Somerset S; Haringey C. rhb. rfm. Also Somerset, Glamorgan, Derbyshire II, Surrey II, Middlesex II, Essex II. Clubs: Hurst, Finchampstead.

FOSTER, MARK RICHARD LINDFIELD (2006-08). b 1.11.1980 Chichester, Sussex. rhb. wk. Club: Falkland.

FOX, ROY (1951-54). b 1.9.1920 Dewsbury, Yorkshire. ed Wheelwright GS, Dewsbury; Bradford TC. rhb. Cap (1951). Also Cheshire. Club: Reading.

FRANCIS, NORMAN KERSHAW (1950). b 19.10.1910 Greenwich, Kent. d 20.8.1996 Hungerford. Also Bedfordshire. Hockey (Bedfordshire). Clubs: Reading, Berkshire Gentlemen.

FRAY, THOMAS DAVID (1997-2006). b 20.9.1979 Epping, Essex. ed Maidenhead C; Cardiff U. rhb. Cap (2005). Also MCCA (ST, u-25), Middlesex II. MCC YC. Clubs: North Maidenhead, Reading.

FRITH, Colonel CYRIL HALSTED (1901-05). b 13.8.1877 Mayfair, London. d 15.4.1946 Sunninghill. ed Charterhouse. wk.

FRITH, JEREMY DAVID JOHN (2006). b 30.10.1977 Epsom, Surrey. ed Mountbatten S, Romsey. rhb. sla. Also Derbyshire II, Gloucestershire II, Channel Isles. Club: Finchampstead.

FRYER, ERNEST HARRAP (1922-24). b 2.5.1903 Henley-on-Thames, Oxfordshire. d 23.5.1972 Guildford, Surrey. ed Wellingborough.

FUSEDALE, NEIL ANDREW (1990-2000). b 11.11.1967 Hendon, London. ed Johannesburg HS; Stellenbosch U, South Africa. rhb. sla. Also Transvaal B, Easterns, Gauteng. Tour: Berkshire to South Africa. Clubs: Maidenhead and Bray, Reading.

GARLICK, JAMES STANLEY (1952). b 30.6.1930 Reading. ed Malvern. rhb. rm. Club: Berkshire Gentlemen.

GARNETT, ERNEST (1907-10). b 5.4.1875 Bromley Cross, Bolton, Lancashire. d 8.9.1950 Reading. ed Charterhouse; CU (Trinity). wk. Also CU. Rackets (CU (3)). Tennis (CU (1)). Club: Wokingham.

GIBB, Dr. JOHN ALDINGTON (1899-1902). b 1869 Jamaica, West Indies. d 11.10.1938 Maidstone, Kent. ed London U; Dublin U; Aberdeen U. lhb. County Club Captain (1900-02). Club: Heathlands.

GIBBONS, JOHN FRANCIS TIVERTON (1958). b 14.12.1934 Highbury, London. ed St Bartholomew's GS, Newbury. rhb. rf. Clubs: Highclere, Berkshire Gentlemen.

GIBSON, ANDREW ERIC (1968-69). b 23.8.1948. ed Highgate. Club: Abingdon.

GIBSON, DAVID (1976-78). b 1.5.1936 Mitcham, Surrey. ed Reading S. rhb. rfm. Also Surrey. Coach Reading School. Club: Old Redingensians.

GIBSON, Rev. HERBERT CYRIL BUTLER (1907). b 11.4.1881 Collingbourne Kingston, Wiltshire. d 16.7.1968 Victoria, British Colombia, Canada. ed Marlborough; OU (Keble). lm. Club: Abingdon.

GIRLING, MICHAEL ARMITAGE (1939). b 2.10.1919 Ipswich, Suffolk. ed Eastbourne C; OU (Brasennose). lhb. Also Oxfordshire.

GOLD, CECIL ARGO (1906). b 3.6.1887 St Pancras, London. d 3.7.1916 Ovillers, La Boiselle, France. ed Eton; OU (Magdalen). Also Middlesex.

GOODLIFFE, Major GUY VERNON (1901-07). b 17.9.1883 Kensington, London. d 29.5.1963 Burnfoot, County Donegal, Ireland. ed Charterhouse; OU (Magdalen). Also OU. Football (Blue (1)).

GOODWORTH, WILLIAM ARTHUR (1961). b 26.3.1923 Liverpool, Lancashire. d 30.9.2001 Emmer Green, Reading. ed Reading S. Club: Reading School Masters.

GORMAN, DAVID BRIAN (1981-88). b 13.8.1955 Havant, Hampshire. rhb. Cap (1984). Tours: Berkshire to New Zealand; to Hong Kong. Club: Reading.

GOVETT, JONATHAN PETER (1995-96). b 22.6.1969 St Germans, Cornwall. ed Brighton Hill S, Basingstoke. rhb. rfm. Also Hampshire II. Club: Basingstoke.

GRAVES, Sir CECIL GEORGE (1922-24). b 4.3.1892 Kensington, London. d 12.1.1957 West Cults, Aberdeenshire. ed Gresham's, Holt; RMC Sandhurst. fm. Also MCC. Club: Royal Berkshire Depot.

GRAY, NEIL CRAIG (1980). b 2.7.1949 Christchurch, Canterbury, New Zealand. rhb. Club: Maidenhead and Bray.

GRAY, PERCY HEATH HOBART (1911-12). b 21.11.1891 Woodland Heights, Richmond, Virginia, United States of America. d 11.10.1971 Digby, Nova Scotia, Canada. ed Bradfield; OU (Queen's). Club: Bradfield School.

GREAVES, GEORGE ROBERT (1913). b 1Q.1877 Kettering, Northamptonshire. d 7.7.1937 Cookham Dean. Also Buckinghamshire.

GREENFIELD, WILLIAM MONTAGUE (1899-05). b 4Q.1871 Reading. ed Reading S; CU (Jesus). Also CU. Club: Reading.

GREGSON-ELLIS, Lt.-Col. GUY SAXON LLEWELLYN (1920-23). b 3.11.1895 Kensington, London. d 12.8.1969 Banbury, Oxfordshire. ed Charterhouse. Also Europeans in India. Club: Wargrave.

GRIFFITHS, DAVID ANDREW (2008). b 10.9.1985 Newport, Isle of Wight. ed Sandown HS. lhb. rfm. Also Hampshire, England u-19. Tour: England u-19 to India. Club: Henley.

GUEST, CHRISTOPHER SHAUN (2008). b 5.7.1984 Wolverhampton, Staffordshire. ed Leeds Metropolitan U. rhb. rmf. Also Worcestershire II, Bradford/Leeds UCCE. Club: Brewood.

GULL, Major FRANCIS WILLIAM LINDLEY (1908). b 3Q.1889 Marylebone, London. d 25.8.1918 Achiet-le-Grand, France. ed Eton; OU (Christ Church).

GUNTER, NEIL EDWARD LLOYD (2000-07). b 12.5.1981 Basingstoke, Hampshire. ed Clere S; Newbury C. lhb. rfm. Cap (2005). Also Derbyshire (ST, u-25), Middlesex II, Northamptonshire II, Derbyshire CB, MCC YC. Club: Falkland.

HABIB, AFTAB (1995-2007). b 7.2.1972 Reading. ed Millfield S; Taunton S. rhb. rm. Cap (1995). Also England (2), England A, Middlesex, Essex (Cap 2002), Leicestershire (Cap 1998), Taranaki, Somerset II, England YC. Tours: England u-19 to Australia; to New Zealand. Berkshire to South Africa. Cousin of Zahid Sadiq (Surrey and Derbyshire). Club: Reading.

HALL, DANNY CHARLES RICHARD (1972-81). b 3.11.1944 Penzance, Cornwall. rhb. Cap (1973). Also Cornwall. Club: Maidenhead and Bray.

HALL, HARRY MARK (1994-2000). b 19.11.1970 Wokingham. ed Ranelagh S; Wye Agricultural C. rhb. sla. Brother of T.L. Club: Finchampstead.

HALL, MICHAEL WELLINGTON (1975-77). b 23.5.1955 Wargrave. ed Harrow. rhb. Club: Boyne Hill.

HALL, THOMAS LEONARD (1995-2002). b 14.6.1969 Wokingham. ed Ranelagh S; Loughborough U. rhb. Basketball (Berkshire). Brother of H.M. Clubs: Finchampstead, Falkland.

HARDING, NORMAN WALTER (1934-36). b 19.3.1916 Woolston, Hampshire. d 25.9.1947 Abingdon. ed Reading S. rhb. rf. Also Kent (Cap 1947). Club: Old Redingensians.

HARE, J. M. (1923).

HARLAND, ADRIAN RODNEY (1962-71). b 7.11.1942 Crowborough, Sussex. ed Reading U. rhb. rfm. Club: Reading.

HARRIS, Colonel HENRY HAY MARSHALL (1913). b 24.12.1878 Godalming, Surrey. d 16.3.1951 Camberley, Surrey. ed Marlborough; RMC Sandhurst. wk. Club: Queens Royal.

HARTLEY, DAVID JOHN BENEDICT (1987-2000). b 28.3.1963 Rushcombe, Reading. ed Ryeish Green S; Lancaster Polytechnic. rhb. lb. Cap (1992). Also MCCA (u-25), Hampshire II, Sussex II. Tours: Berkshire to New Zealand; to South Africa. Clubs: Reading, Three Bridges, Old Hill.

HARTRIDGE, PAUL (1980). b 29.8.1957 Windsor. lhb. rfm. Club: Reading.

HARVEY, JOHN FRANK (1978-87). b 27.9.1939 Barnwell, Cambridgeshire. d 20.8.2003 Bradfield. ed Cambridge City TC. rhb. ob. County Club Captain (1982-86). Cap (1980). Also Derbyshire (Cap 1968), MCC, MCCA (BHC), Cambridgeshire, MCC Groundstaff. Coach Bradfield College. Clubs: Falkland, Sonning.

HARVEY, NICHOLAS PAUL (1993). b 21.11.1973 Ascot. ed Forest CS; Loughborough U. rhb. wk. Also Essex II, Lancashire II, Middlesex II, Leicestershire II, NAYC. Club: Reading.

HAWKSWORTH, GEORGE MARK (1909-28). b 17.2.1880 Aylestone Park, Leicestershire. Also MCCA (NvS, sc), Devon. County Club Professional. Coach Bradfield College.

HEAD, MALCOLM ARTHUR (1975-79). b 5.9.1953 Purley, Surrey. rhb. wk. Club: Reading.

HEADLEY, GARY TYRONE (1988-94). b 5.9.1966 Reading. ed Llanedeym HS. rhb. rm. Also Derbyshire II, Glamorgan II, Middlesex II, MCC YC. Club: Shepherds Bush (pro), Finchampstead.

HEAPE, EDWARD HENRY WALTER (1972-77). b 15.2.1946 Burton-upon-Trent, Staffordshire. lhb. sla. Also Wiltshire, Northamptonshire II, Derbyshire II. Club: Swindon BR.

HEARNE, THOMAS JOHN (1922-23). b 3.7.1887 Ealing, Middlesex. d 25.5.1947 Poole, Dorset. lm. Also Middlesex. Grandson of T. (Middlesex), son of G.F. (Middlesex).

HEASMAN, Dr. WILLIAM GRATWICKE (1896). b 9.12.1862 Angmering, Sussex. d 25.1.1934 Upperton, Eastbourne, Sussex. rhb. rf. Also Sussex, Norfolk. Tour: Philadelphians to Bermuda. Grandfather of M.R.G.Earls-Davis (Somerset). Club: Wokingham.

HENDERSON, Hon. ARNOLD (1899-1903). b 1.7.1883 Norwood Green, Middlesex. d 12.3.1933 Writtle Park, Chelmsford, Essex. ed Wellington. wk. Brother of E.B.B.

HENDERSON, Hon. ERIC BRAND BUTLER (1902). b 26.9.1884 Norwood Green, Middlesex. d 18.12.1953 Faccombe Manor, Andover, Hampshire. ed Eton. Brother of A.

HERMON, JOHN VICTOR (later **HERMON-WILSON**) (1924). b 22.11.1905 Nantwich, Cheshire. d 9.9.1943 Salerno, Italy. ed Harrow. Club: Wargrave.

HESELTINE, PHILLIP JOHN (1988-89). b 21.6.1960 Skipton, Yorkshire. ed Holgate GS; OU (Keble). rhb. rm. Also OU (1), Lincolnshire, Derbyshire II. Tour: Berkshire to New Zealand. Brother of P.A.W. (Sussex). Club: Wokingham.

HEWAN, GETHYN ELLIOTT (1946). b 23.12.1916 Merchiston, Edinburgh, Midlothian, Scotland. d 1.7.1988 Chertsey, Surrey. ed Marlborough; CU (Clare). rhb ob. Also CU (1), Public Schools. Tour: MCC to Denmark. Hockey (CU (3), Captain 1938).

HEWETT, MICHAEL JOHN (1981-82). b 28.8.1950 Hampstead, London. ed Beckenham and Penge GS. rhb. rmf. Also Gloucestershire (lo), Worcestershire II. Club: Wallingford.

HEYN, PETER DAVID (1981). b 26.6.1945 Colombo, Ceylon. ed St Peters C. lhb. rm. Also Sri Lanka (odi, 2), Ceylon, Mercantile Cricket Association. Tours: Sri Lanka to India; to Pakistan. Club: Richmond.

HILL, Lieut.-Colonel. CHARLES GLENCAIRN ('ANDREW') (1910-13). b 22.9.1872 Winchester, Hampshire. d 26.6.1915 Pas de Calais, France. ed Haileybury. Also Northumberland.

HILL, Captain ELIOT FOLEY (1896-98). b 12.1877 Mayfair, London. ed Wellington. Club: Newbury.

HILLARY, ANTHONY AYLMER (1954-62). b 28.8.1926 Shenfield, Essex. d 20.6.1991 Truro, Cornwall. ed Brentwood S; CU (Jesus). rhb. ob. Cap (1958). Also CU, Essex II. Master-in-charge of cricket Abingdon S. Clubs: Abingdon, Reading.

HINCHCLIFFE, MARTIN (1982-83). b 1.12.1960 Cinderford, Gloucestershire. ed Ascot S. rhb. rfm. Also Leicestershire II, NAYC. Clubs: Ascot, Reading.

HINDE, Brigadier HAROLD MONTAGUE (1921-32). b 24.8.1895 Southsea, Hampshire. d 16.11.1965 Santa Margherita Liguse, Italy. ed Wellington; Blundells. rhb. rf. Also MCCA (fc, NvS), Egypt. Rugby (Richmond). Brother of W.H.R. Club: RASC.

HINDE, WILLIAM HENRY ROUSSEAU (1913-14). b 2Q.1891 Southsea, Hampshire. d 22.10.1918 Headingley, Yorkshire. ed Wellington; OU (Oriel). Hockey (OU (Blue)). Brother of H.M.

HINDS, JEREMY NIGEL PARKER (2006). b 16.11.1970 Guildford, Surrey. rhb. ob. Club: Avorians.

HODGKINS, HENRY JOSEPH JORDAN (1911). b 11.11.1868 Cheltenham, Gloucestershire. d 24.6.1952 Dorchester, Dorset. ed Trent C. lhb. lm. Also Gloucestershire, Bedfordshire. Club: Faringdon.

HODGSON, CHARLES PAUL ROLLS (1996). b 15.12.1977 Guildford, Surrey. ed Wellington; Durham U. lhb. lb. Also Surrey II, Essex II. ESCA. Brother of T.P. (Essex), J.S. (CU) and M.A. (Surrey II), great-nephew of N.A.Knox (England, Surrey). Club: Weybridge.

HODGSON, JAMES (1993-98). b 28.3.1972 Reading. ed Ranelagh S; Loughborough U. rhb. lb. Cap (1995). Also Nottinghamshire II, Kent CB, England YC. England u-19 to New Zealand. Clubs: The Mote, Wokingham.

HOLDSWORTH, Lieut.-Colonel ARTHUR MERVYN (1908-14). b 5.11.1875 Newton Abbot, Devon. d 7.7.1916 Etaples, Boulogne, France. ed Harrow; CU (Trinity Hall). Club: Royal Berks Regiment.

HOOPER, KENNETH MORTON DOUGLAS (1956-57). b 9.1927 Beckenham, Kent. d 1.11.2007 Oxford. ed Shrewsbury, OU (Worcester). rm.

HOPCROFT, HARRY EDGAR (1927). b 3Q.1896 Kidderminster, Worcestershire. ed Reading S. Club: Caversham.

HORNER, ROBERT WILLIAM (1994-99). b 20.1.1967 Liskeard, Cornwall. ed Dargaville HS, New Zealand. rhb. wk. Club: Ilminster.

HOURD, JOHN HENRY (1959). b 10.11.1930 Southall, Middlesex. ed Southall S. rhb.rm. Club: Southall.

HOUSEGO, DANIEL MARK (2006). b 6.10.1988 Windsor. ed Oratory S. rhb. lb. Also Middlesex II, ESCA. Club: Reading.

HOWARD, Canon FRANCIS JAMES (1905-06). b 4Q.1877 Dudley, Worcestershire. d 13.6.1949 Burgerspital, Basle, Switzerland. ed Bedford Modern S; OU (Keble). Club: Reading.

HOWARD, Captain PERCY (1909-26). b 4Q.1888 Newbury. wk. Club: Newbury.

HOWES, ROBERT C. (1951). b 2.9.1928 Hamilton, Ontario, Canada. ed Maidenhead County BS. rhb. rmf. Club: Maidenhead and Bray.

HOWITT, RICHARD WILLIAM JOHN (2003-04). b 17.8.1977 Grantham, Lincolnshire. ed Denstone; Swansea U; CU (Homerton). lhb. rm. Also CU (1), MCCA (ST), England CB, Lincolnshire, Bedfordshire, Nottinghamshire II, Kent II, Essex II, NAYC. Club: Bourne.

HUBBARD, WILTON OLDHAM (1908-09). b 2Q.1876 Brentford, Middlesex. d 17.11.1918 Guernsey. ed Tonbridge. Club: Reading.

HUBBLE, HENRY GEORGE CHARLTON (1935-39). b 23.12.1909 Hollingbourne, Kent. d 22.3.85 Tunbridge Wells, Kent. ed Reading U. Rugby (UAU). Clubs: Reading University, The Mote.

HUGONIN, Captain FRANCIS EDGAR (1935). b 16.8.1897 Kensington, London. d 5.3.1967 Stainton-in-Cleveland House, Yorkshire. ed Eastbourne C. rhb. wk. Also Essex, Army, Straits Settlement. Clubs: I Zingari, Berkshire Gentlemen.

HUMAN, JOHN HANBURY (1928-34). b 13.1.1912 Gosforth, Northumberland. d 22.7.1991 Sydney, New South Wales, Australia. ed Repton; CU (Clare). rhb. lb. Also CU (3, Captain 1934), Middlesex. Tours: MCC to India and Ceylon; to Australia and New Zealand. Brother of R.H.C. Club: Repton School.

HUMAN, ROGER HENRY CHARLES (1925-34). b 11.5.1909 Gosforth, Northumberland. d 21.11.1942 Bangalore, India. ed Repton; CU (Emmanuel). rhb. rm. Also CU (2), Worcestershire, Oxfordshire, Public Schools. Tour: MCC to India (cancelled). Football (CU (1)). Brother of J.H. Club: Repton School.

HUNT, THOMAS MARK CHAMBERS (1906-10). b 1Q.1872 Wortley, Yorkshire. d 30.12.1950 Wallingford. ed Bedford Modern S. Club: Reading.

HUNTER, JOHN CHARLES (1902-03). b 24.6.1884 Beech Hill, Bradfield. d 1.6.1904 Rawalpindi, India. ed Bradfield, RMC Sandhurst. Club: Bradfield College.

HUTCHINGS, WILLIAM EDWARD COLEBROOKE (1901). b 31.5.1879 Southborough, Kent. d 8.3.1948 Prees, Shropshire. ed Tonbridge. rhb. Also Kent, Worcestershire. Brother of F.V. (Kent) and K.L. (Kent), nephew of E.L.Colebrooke (OU). Club: Abingdon.

HUTSON, HENRY WOLSELEY (1899-1906). b 14.3.1868 Georgetown, Demerara, British Guiana. d 25.3.1916 Cottenham Park, Wimbledon, Surrey. ed privately; CU (Jesus). Also CU.

HUXLEY, BARRY MARTIN (1975). b 6.1.1950 Windlesham, Surrey. ed Bradfield. rhb. Also NAYC. Club: Bradfield Waifs.

IGGLESDEN, ALAN PAUL (1999). b 8.10.1964 Farnborough, Kent. ed Churchills SS, Westerham. rhb. rfm. Also England (3), Kent (Cap 1989), Western Province, Boland, Impala. Tours: England to West Indies; England A to Zimbabwe; Kent to Zimbabwe. Club: Unattached.

INGRAM, CHARLES (1949).

INGRAM, FRANCIS MANNING (1896-1903). b 6.11.1864 Westminster, London. d 10.6.1933 Ockford Wood, Godalming, Surrey. ed Winchester; OU (Magdalen). Also Gentlemen of Sussex. Football (England (3), OU (2), Corinthians). Club: Free Foresters.

INGRAM, THOMAS (1955-57). rhb. wk. Cap. Also British Police. Football (Berkshire Police). Club: Reading.

IREMONGER, GUY THORNHILL (1920). b 4Q.1889 Bradfield.

JACK, THOMAS W. (1959-66). rhb. ob. Clubs: Bracknell, Berkshire Gentlemen.

JACKSON, BARRY SCOTT (1989-94). b 13.9.1966 Maidenhead. ed Desborough. rhb. rmf. Also Somerset II. Clubs: Bearwood, Boyne Hill.

JACKSON, JOHN WILLOUGHBY (1938). b 4.10.1916 Cookham. d 9.2000 Salisbury, Wiltshire. ed Eastbourne C; CU (St Catharine's). Also MCCA (sc), Buckinghamshire.

JACKSON, KENNETH LESLIE TATTERSALL (1938-46). b 17.11.1913 Shanghai, China. d 21.3.1982 Hinton St George, Somerset. ed Rugby; OU (Trinity). Also OU (1). Rugby (Scotland (4), OU (3, Captain 1935)).

JAMES, ARTHUR EDWIN (1899-1900). b 2Q.1873 Newbury. Professional.

JAMES, ROBERT MICHAEL (1954-71). b 2.10.1934 Wokingham. ed St John's Leatherhead; CU (Trinity). Cap (1962). Also CU (3), MCCA (fc, sc), Wellington, Public Schools. Father of T.M.H. Club: Newbury.

JAMES, TIMOTHY MICHAEL HOWARD (1982-86). b 7.2.1960 Beaconsfield, Buckinghamshire. ed Harrow; Reading U. rhb. rm. Cap (1986). Also Ghana, Surrey II. Tour: Berkshire to Hong Kong. Son of R.M. Clubs: Sonning, Wokingham.

JARRETT, GLYN BRIAN (1966). b 2Q.1936 Orsett, Essex. ed Palmers S, Grays, Essex; OU (Pembroke).

JENNINGS, WILLIAM HENRY (1931-32). b 2Q.1893 Wallingford. Clubs: Boyne Hill, Berkshire Gentlemen.

JEWELL, GUY ALONZO FREDERICK WILLIAM (1938). b 6.10.1916 Axford, Hampshire. d 23.12.1965 Basingstoke, Hampshire. ed Reading U. lhb. sla. Also Hampshire. Club: Basingstoke.

JOHNSON, RICHARD LEONARD (2008). b 29.12.1974 Chertsey, Surrey. ed Sunbury Manor S. rhb. rfm. Cap (2008). Also England (3), England (odi, 10), Middlesex (Cap 1995), Somerset (Cap 2001). Tours: England to Bangladesh; England A to Bangladesh; to India; Middlesex to Ireland; Nottinghamshire to South Africa; England u-19 to Bangladesh; to Sri Lanka. Cricket Coach Wellington College. Club: Sunbury.

JOHNSON, RICHARD NEVILLE (1960-69). b 2Q.1943 Maidenhead. ed Wellington; CU (Magdalene). Club: Bracknell.

JOHNSTON, DAVID (1960-80). b 17.4.1943 Blackpool, Lancashire. rhb. lb. Cap (1970). Also MCCA (BHC). Tour: Berkshire to Hong Kong. Club: Reading.

JONES, JEFFERSON HARCOURT (1972-94). b 6.1.1954 Christchurch, Barbados. ed Christchurch HS. rhb. rfm. Cap (1975). Also MCCA (odm). Tours: Berkshire to New Zealand; to South Africa; to Hong Kong. Club: Reading.

JONES, MATTHEW ALAN (2006). b 1.9.1988 Cardiff, Glamorgan. ed Forest S. lhb. ob. Also Glamorgan II. Son of A.L. (Glamorgan). Club: Finchampstead.

JONES, PETER (1959). b 7.2.1930 Swansea, Glamorgan. d 2.4.1990 Wandsworth, Surrey. ed Bishops Gore S, Swansea; CU (Queen's).

KAYE, Colonel COLIN MICHAEL SUTTON (1961). b 20.7.1943 Wakefield, Yorkshire. ed Harrow; RMA Sandhurst. Also Army.

KEFFORD, HARRY KINGSLEY (1923-24). b 30.5.1900 Faversham, Kent. d 18.12.1975 Chaddleworth, Newbury. ed Wellingborough; CU (St John's).

KENDRICK, NEIL MICHAEL (1997-98). b 11.11.1967 Bromley, Kent. ed Wilsons GS. rhb. sla. Also Surrey, Glamorgan, Surrey CB, NAYC, England YC. Tours: Glamorgan to Zimbabwe; MCC to Canada. Club: Banstead.

KILLICK, HERBERT STANLEY CALEB (1947). b 15.1.1911 Fulham, Middlesex. d 2.1.1985 Gerrards Cross, Buckinghamshire. ed St Paul's.

KINGSLEY, DAVID CHARLES (1947-48). ed Beaumont S. ob. Also Public Schools, Southern Schools. Rugby (East Midlands, Bedfordshire).

KINGSMILL, RICHARD GEORGE JOHN (1937). b 1.11.1911 East Preston, Sussex. d 9.11.1996 Hales, Norwich, Norfolk. ed RMC Sandhurst. Club: RASC.

KINGSTON, STEVEN CHARLES (1979-86). b 21.12.1955 Valetta, Malta. rhb. rfm. Club: Finchampstead.

KINGSTONE, JAMES HOWARD (2004-05). b 10.2.1982 Reading. ed St Crispin's, Wokingham. rhb. wk. Clubs: Teddington, Finchampstead.

KIRBY, GEOFFREY NORMAN GEORGE (1954). b 6.11.1923 Reading. d 7.2.2004 Nettlebed, Oxfordshire. ed Reading S. rhb. wk. Cap (1954). Also Surrey. Club: Reading.

KNAPP, Lieut.-Colonel THOMAS HENRY (1932-38). b 14.5.1913 Reading. d 25.2.1979 Reading. ed Pangbourne C; RMC Sandhurst. Cap (1933). Also Army. Clubs: Dorsetshire Regiment, RMC.

KNIGHT, GEOFFREY PHILIP (1970-82). b 14.6.1947 Pinner, Middlesex. rhb. lb. Cap (1980). Club: Reading.

KRABBE, PETER GORDON (1935-39). b 2.9.1916 St German, Cornwall. d 27.5.1940 St Venant, France. ed Stowe; OU (Trinity). Club: Berkshire Gentlemen.

KYNASTON, WILLIAM FREDERICK (1909). b 1Q.1879 Aston, Warwickshire. Club: Reading.

LAMBERT, THOMAS LUKE (1999-2008). b 9.5.1981 Ascot. ed St Windsor Boys S; Cardiff U. rhb. rmf. Cap (2005). Also MCCA (ST,od,lo,u-25), Cardiff UCCE. Clubs: Datchet, Slough, Pentyrch, Henley.

LAMSDALE, PETER MARTIN (1995-99). b 11.3.1971 Shifnal, Shropshire. ed Regis S. rhb. rfm. Also Surrey II. Tour: Berkshire to South Africa. Club: Reading.

LANE, MARK GEOFFREY (1995-2001). b 26.1.1968 Aldershot, Hampshire. ed Oak Farm, Farnborough. rhb. wk. Cap (1998). Also Surrey II, Hampshire II. Tour: Berkshire to South Africa. Clubs: Guildford, Weybridge.

LANGDALE, GEORGE RICHMOND (1952-63). b 11.3.1916 Thornaby-on-Tees, Yorkshire. d 24.4.2002 Welbeck, Worksop, Nottinghamshire. ed Nottingham U. lhb. ob. County Club Captain (1956-59). Cap (1952). Also Derbyshire, Somerset, Army, MCCA (sc), Norfolk. Club: Camberley.

LANGLEY, IAN JAMES (1964-65). b 7.10.1940 Maidenhead. ed Maidenhead GS. rhb. rfm. Brother of S.W. Club: Maidenhead and Bray.

LANGLEY, STEWART WILLIAM (1965-73). b 24.5.1939 Maidenhead. ed Maidenhead GS. rhb. ob. Brother of I.J. Club: Maidenhead and Bray.

LARKCOM, ALAN HEDLEY (1972-74). b 2.11.1945 Ashampstead. lhb. rm. Also Surrey II. Club: Newbury.

LATCHMAN, RANJIT KARAMCHAND (1980-81). b 16.11.1945 Kingston, Jamaica. rhb. Club: Northwood.

LAWRENCE, H. C. (1952). Club: Berkshire Gentlemen.

LAWRENCE, TERENCE PATRICK (1947). b 26.4.1910 Waltham Abbey, Essex. d 7.1.1989 Fawley, Wantage. ed Uppingham; CU (Corpus Christi). rhb. lb. Also Essex, Hertfordshire.

LAY, WILLIAM FRANCIS (1902). b 4Q.1878 Abingdon. Club: Abingdon.

LEONARD (1909).

LETTS, PHILIP EDWARD (1938-46). b 12.1.1912 Conway, Caernarvonshire. d 14.3.1977 Baschurch, Shropshire. ed Christs Hospital S.; OU (Magdalen). Clubs: Henley, Sussex Martlets.

LEWINGTON, PETER JOHN (1967-96). b 30.1.1950 Finchampstead. ed Ranelagh. rhb. ob. Cap (1968). Also Warwickshire, Taranaki, MCCA (BHC), Surrey II, Hampshire II. Tours: Berkshire to New Zealand; to Hong Kong; Robins to South Africa; MCC to Bangladesh; to Canada. Professional Wellington College. Clubs: Finchampstead, Walsall.

LEWIS, ARTHUR HAMILTON (1931-37). b 16.9.1901 Maseru, Basutoland. d 23.8.1980 Heavitree, Devon. ed King William's C, Isle of Man; CU (Jesus). rhb. Also Hampshire. Clubs: Cryptics, Hampshire Hogs.

LEWIS, HAROLD LOGAN (1924-46). b 18.4.1895 High Wycombe, Buckinghamshire. d 2.6.1978 Waltham St Lawrence. rhb. County Club Captain (1933). County Club Honorary Secretary (1945-72). Hockey (Berkshire). Clubs: Huntley and Palmers, Berkshire Gentlemen.

LICKLEY, MARTIN GREGORY (1981-93). b 15.8.1957 Windsor. ed Trevelyn SS. rhb. rm. Cap (1982). Also Middlesex II, Gloucestershire II. Tours: Berkshire to New Zealand; to Hong Kong. Clubs: Finchampstead, Slough.

LINCOLN-GORDON, PETER (1949-52). b 1926 Bengal, India. d 18.4.2003 Naivasha, Kenya. ed Reading S. rhb. rm. Club: Reading.

LISTON, DAVID (1971-81). b 29.6.1949 Lambeth, London. ed Archbishop Tenison's S, Kennington. rhb. sla. Clubs: Bracknell, Brent.

LLOYD, ERNEST BEDFORD (1948-49). b 3Q.1909 Swindon, Wiltshire. Also Wiltshire.

LOCKHART, JOHN HAROLD BRUCE (1911-12). b 4.3.1889 Beith, Ayrshire, Scotland. d 4.6.1956 Marylebone, London. ed Sedbergh S; CU (Jesus). rhb. lbg. Also CU (2), Scotland (2). Rugby (Scotland (2), CU, London Scottish). Father of R.B. (CU), brother-in-law of H.Brougham (OU).

LOVEDAY, GARY EDWARD (1985-2000). b 15.4.1964 Eton Wick, Windsor. ed Emmbrook S; Loughborough U. rhb. rm. County Club Captain (1996-2000). Cap (1988). Also MCCA (lo). Tours: Berkshire to New Zealand; to South Africa. Club: Finchampstead.

LOWE, HENRY ST ALBAN (1902). b 2Q.1875 Kearsley, Lancashire. d 9.3.1943 Henley-on-Thames, Oxfordshire. ed Shrewsbury; CU (Trinity). Football (CU (Blue)).

LUTHER, Major ALAN CHARLES GRENVILLE (1926-27). b 17.9.1880 Kensington, London. d 23.6.1961 Staplemead, Curland, Somerset. ed Rugby; RMC Sandhurst. rhb. County Club Honorary Secretary (1927-28). Also Sussex, Army. Tour: MCC to Egypt.

McCARTHY, JOSEPH CORNELIUS (1900). b 1Q.1876 Gosport, Hampshire. ed Reading S. Club: Sonning.

McCONNELL, WILLIAM HENRY (1934-35). b 2.9.1902 Corbolis, Northern Ireland. d 1Q.1976 Slough, Buckinghamshire. ed Reading S. Football (Northern Ireland (8), Slough Town, Reading). Club: Reading.

McDONALD, JOHN ALEXANDER (1999). b 28.4.1967 Wokingham. ed Presentation C, Reading. rhb. sla. Club: Wokingham.

MACKENZIE, PERCY ALEC (1947-48). b 5.10.1918 Canterbury, Kent. d 1.1.1989 Rye, Sussex. rhb. lbg. Also Hampshire, RAF, Kent II. Club: Reading.

McLEAN, JONATHAN JAMES (2008). b 11.7.1980 Johannesburg, South Africa. ed St Stitian's S, Capre Town. rhb. rm. Also South Africa Academy, Western Province, Hampshire. Club: Henley.

McLEAN, W. R. (1929). Club: Reading.

MAGILL, MICHAEL DESMOND PONSONBY (1939). b 28.9.1915 Sevenoaks, Kent. d 5.9.1940 Filey, Yorkshire. ed Eton; OU (Brasennose). rhb. rfm. Also OU, Army. Tour: Oxford and Cambridge U to Jamaica. Club: I Zingari.

MAHONEY, ALEXANDER JOHN (1975-76). b 30.1.1947 Invercargill, Southland, New Zealand. rhb. sla. Cap (1975). Also Southland, Wairarapa. Club: Reading.

MARC, KERVIN (1996-98). b 9.1.1975 Mon Repos, St Lucia, West Indies. ed Oratory S; Central St Martin CAD. rhb. rf. Also Middlesex, Central Districts, MCCA (ST), Derbyshire II, Kent II, Worcestershire II, Middlesex CB, Surrey CB, British Universities, MCC YC. Clubs: Stevenage, Shepherds Bush.

MARTIN, JOHN DONALD (1972). b 23.12.1941 Oxford. ed Magdalen College S; OU (St Edmund Hall). Also OU (3, Captain 1965), Somerset, Oxfordshire. Hockey (CU (Blue)). Tour: MCC to South America. Club: Cowley St John.

MARTINEAU, Sir PHILIP HUBERT (1905). b 28.10.1862 St Pancras, London. d 7.10.1944 Wentworth, Surrey. ed Harrow; CU (Trinity). lfm. Also MCC. Father of H.M. (Leveson-Gower XI), uncle of L. (CU).

MASON, JAMES ERNEST (1905). b 29.10.1876 Blackheath, Kent. d 8.2.1938 South Beddington, Wallington, Surrey. ed Tonbridge. rhb. Also Kent. Brother of J.R. (Kent).

MASSEY, ALAN (1963). b 28.9.1935 Bolton, Lancashire. d 27.10.1994 Reading. ed Bolton GS; Manchester U. rhb. rfm. Club: Reading.

MASSEY, SIMON NIGEL CRAIG (1987-88). b 14.10.1961 Newcastle-under-Lyme, Staffordshire. ed Calthorpe S. rhb. ob. Also Derbyshire II, Northamptonshire II, Warwickshire II, Hampshire II, Worcestershire II. Tour: Berkshire to New Zealand. Son of G. (Staffordshire). Club: Finchampstead.

MATTHEWS, Lieut.-Colonel ERNEST DUDLEY (1904-07). b 8.5.1875 Sandhurst. d 6.1.1944 Stanley Internment Camp, Hong Kong. ed Rossall; Yorkshire Engineering C. Also Hong Kong. Clubs: Royal Artillery, Reading.

MATTHEWS, FREDERICK ROY (1977-79). b 7.4.1952 Newton Abbot, Devon. sla. Club: Maidenhead and Bray.

MATTHEWS, JOHN CECIL GAD (1905). b 3.10.1875 Stoke Bishop, Gloucestershire. d 1.5.1940 Honiton, Devon. ed Winchester. Club: Maidenhead.

MAULE, Wing Commander ERIC HERBERT (1934-35). b 15.5.1917 Barnet, Hertfordshire. d 3.5.1996 Reading. ed Reading S. Rugby (Berkshire). Club: Reading School.

MAURICE, Lieut.-Colonel DAVID BLAKE (1910). b 24.12.1866 Reading. d 4.12.1925 Reading. ed Uppingham. Brother of S.H., son-in-law of James Simonds. Clubs: Reading, Royal Berkshire Regiment.

MAURICE, SIDNEY HENRY (1896). b 16.9.1869 Reading. d 10.5.1898 Salisbury, Rhodesia. ed Marlborough; CU (Trinity). Brother of D.B. Clubs: Hurst, Reading.

MAXWELL, CHRISTOPHER BAILLIE (1895). b 10.6.1867 Ponsonby, Auckland, New Zealand. Club: Reading Biscuit Factory.

MAY, JAMES (1900). b 4Q.1861 Wokingham. Club: Wokingham.

MAY, JOHN WHITELEY HOWARD (1950-56). b 5.11.1932 Reading. d 23.10.1988 Fulham, London. ed Charterhouse. rhb. Cap (1954). Also Public Schools. Brother of P.B.H. Club: Old Carthusians.

MAY, PETER BARKER HOWARD (1946). b 31.12.1929 The Mount, Reading. d 27.12.1994 Liphook, Hampshire. ed Charterhouse; CU (Pembroke). Also England (66, Captain (41)), Surrey (Captain 1957-62, Cap 1960), CU, Combined Services. Football (CU (2)). Brother of J.W.H., son-in-law of A.H.H.Gilligan (England, Sussex). Club: Charterhouse School.

MENCE, JOSEPH ALAN (1946-65). b 21.4.1921 Hampstead, London. ed Aldenham. rhb. lb. County Club Captain (1954-55). Cap (1947). Hockey (Berkshire). Father of M.D. Club: Berkshire Gentlemen.

MENCE, MICHAEL DAVID (1961-82). b 13.4.1944 Newbury. ed Bradfield. lhb. rm. County Club Captain (1976-78). Cap (1961). Also Warwickshire, Gloucestershire, MCCA (BHC). Tour MCC to Bangladesh. Son of J.A. Clubs: Bradfield Waifs, Smethwick.

MERCER, DAVID JEREMY MATTHEW (1989-94). b 7.5.1962 Warrington, Lancashire. ed Bishop Wordsworth S. rhb. ob. occ wk. Also Wiltshire, Bedfordshire, England Amateur XI. Club: Reading.

MERCER, DONALD (1901). b 11.12.1869 Edenfield, Lancashire. ed Trent C; CU (Pembroke). Football (CU (Blue)). Club: Abingdon.

MERRETT, PETER A. (1961). b 3Q. 1938 Reading. ed Reading S. rhb. rm. Also United States of America. Club: Reading.

METCALFE, Sir FREDERIC WILLIAM (1908-10). b 4.12.1886 Ceylon. d 3.6.1965 London. ed Wellington; CU (Sidney Sussex).

MILLS, PERCY THOMAS (1931). b 7.5.1879 Cheltenham, Gloucestershire. d 8.12.1950 Abingdon. rhb. rm. Also Gloucestershire. FC Umpire. Coach Radley College.

MILLS, SYDNEY LAWRENCE (1920). b 1Q.1893 Walsall, Staffordshire. Club: Wokingham.

MITCHELL, Colonel PETER ANTHONY (1959). b 10.6.1932 Cox Green, Maidenhead. ed Ampleforth; RMA Woolwich. rhb. ra. Also Hong Kong, Army. Clubs: Old Amplefordians, Free Foresters.

MOHAMMAD AMJAD (1987). b 14.12.1961 Pakistan. rhb. rm.

MOLE, CHARLES WILLIAM (1931-38). b 19.11.1912 Reading. d 1.9.1944 Gradara, Pesaro, Italy. ed Marlborough; CU (Pembroke). Club: Berkshire Amateurs.

MOON, VERNON RICHARD (1947). b 11.9.1910 Farnham, Surrey. d 10.1993 Reading. Also RAF.

MORBEY, Dr. RONALD D. (1946-53). b 3Q.1925 Reading. ed Reading S; St Mary's Hospital. rhb. rfm. Cap (1947). Club: Reading.

MORDAUNT, DAVID JOHN (1964-74). b 24.8.1937 Chelsea, London. ed Wellington. rhb. rm. Cap (1964). Also Sussex, MCCA (sc). Tours: MCC to North America; to South America. Grandson of G.J. (Kent), great-grandson of J.N. (MCC). Club: Horsham.

MORDT, BJORN HAAKEN DAVID (2003-08). b 29.6.1978 Mutare, Zimbabwe. ed Reading S. rhb. wk. County Club Captain (2007-08). Cap (2005). Clubs: Reading, Henley.

MORGAN, Dr. MICHAEL NAUGHTON (1950-59). b 15.5.1932 Marylebone, London. ed Marlborough; CU (Downing). rhb. rfm. Cap (1950). Also CU (1).

MORGAN, PETER (1971). b 14.9.1942 Isleworth, Middlesex. lhb. Club: Slough.

MORRES, Major EDWARD REDMOND (1897-1900). b 3.9.1873 Wokingham. d 27.12.1954 Guernsey. ed Winchester; OU (Magdalen). Also Dorset, Guernsey. Brother of H.F.M., son of H.R., nephew of H.R. and R.E.

MORRES, HUGH FREDERICK MICHAEL (1897-1923). b 8.7.1876 Wokingham. d 28.1.1934 Swanage, Dorset. ed Winchester; OU (Keble). rhb. rfm. Also OU, Dorset, Buckinghamshire, Guernsey. Brother of E.R., son of H.R., nephew of H.R. and R.E.

MORRIS, JAMES CALUM (2002-08). b 17.1.1985 Welwyn Garden City, Hertfordshire. ed Bradfield; Durham U. rhb. lb. Cap (2008). Also British U. (Captain), Durham UCCE, Surrey II, Sussex II, Glamorgan II, Leicestershire II, Northamptonshire II, Hampshire II. Brother of R.K. (Hampshire). Club: Falkland.

MOSS, Squadron-Leader EDWARD HENRY (1938-39). b 25.5.1911 Godden Green, Kent. d 31.3.1944 Rimbach, Fulda, Germany. ed Malvern; OU (Trinity). rhb. Cap (1939). Also OU, Kent II. Golf (South, OU). Brother of R.F. (Europeans).

MOULSDALE, JOHN GRAHAM BLACKWALL (1948-50). b 3.8.1926 Stafford. ed Shrewsbury; CU (Emmanuel). rhb. Club: Berkshire Gentlemen.

MUNDY, HARRY JOHN C. (1930-31). b 26.11.1903 Reading. d 2Q.1980 Reading. Club: Denham Park (pro).

MURDOCH-COZENS, ALAN JAMES (1911-13). b 17.9.1893 Wallingford. d 23.7.1970 Malvern, Worcestershire. ed Brighton C. Also Sussex.

MURPHY, HUGH EDWARD McLAUGHLIN (1959-64). b 7.1942 Surrey. ed Bradfield; CU (Christ's). rhb. wk. Cap (1963). Also Surrey II, Southern Schools.

MURRAY, KEVIN STUART (1984-92). b 3.1.1963 Brisbane, Queensland, Australia. lhb. Also Somerset II. Tours: Berkshire to New Zealand; to Hong Kong. Club: Maidenhead and Bray.

MYLES, SIMON DAVID (1995-2000). b 2.6.1966 Mansfield, Nottinghamshire. ed King George V S, Hong Kong. rhb. rm. Cap (1995). Also Sussex, Warwickshire, Hong Kong, MCCA, Cumberland, Staffordshire, Derbyshire II, Somerset II. Tour: Berkshire to South Africa. Club: Wokingham.

NARES, WILLIAM OWEN (1895-1900). b 2Q.1859 Haverfordwest, Pembrokeshire. d 26.3.1928 Kimpton, Hertfordshire. ed Rossall; OU (Jesus). County Club Honorary Secretary (1896-1901). Stepfather of E.J.Wickens. Clubs: Reading, Sonning.

NASH, PHILIP GEOFFREY ELWIN (1924-30). b 20.9.1906 Accrington, Lancashire. d 8.12.1982 Old Basing, Basingstoke, Hampshire. ed St Paul's; OU (Worcester). rhb. rm. Also OU. Rugby Fives (OU (1)).

NAYLOR, STEVEN PAUL (2002-08). b 14.3.1977 Billingham, Durham. ed Northfield S, Stockton; Billingham C. rhb. rfm. Cap (2005). Also MCCA, Buckinghamshire, Durham II, Middlesex II, Nottinghamshire II, Surrey II, Northamptonshire II, Huntingdonshire, MCC YC. Club: Avorians.

NEAME, Colonel BERNARD (1927). b 12.5.1883 Bromley, Kent. d 29.10.1954 Brailsford, Ashbourne, Derbyshire. ed Harrow. Club: Abingdon.

NEATE, FRANCIS WEBB (Senior) (1932-33). b 28.6.1911 Newbury. d 13.12.1982 Kew, London. ed Cheltenham; OU (Brasenose). rhb. rm. Father of F.W. (jun) and P.W. Clubs: Berkshire Gentlemen, Richmond.

NEATE, FRANCIS WEBB (Junior) (1958-79). b 13.5.1940 Newbury. ed St Paul's; OU (Brasenose). rhb. County Club Captain (1971-75). Cap (1959). Also OU (2), MCCA (sc), Surrey II. Brother of P.W., son of F.W. (sen). Clubs: Falkland, Richmond.

NEATE, PATRICK WHISTLER (1964-79). b 2.5.1946 Newbury. ed St Paul's; OU (Brasenose). lhb. rm. Cap (1967). Also OU. Brother of F.W. (jun), son of F.W. (sen). Clubs: Falkland, Richmond.

NEPEAN, Sir CHARLES EVAN MOLYNEUX YORKE (1895-1914) (registered as CE Nepean at birth). (became 5th Baron Nepean in 1903). b 24.3.1867 Horncastle, Lincolnshire. d 1.1.1953 Uplyme, Lyme Regis, Dorset. ed Winchester. rm. County Club Captain (1903-14). Club: Royal Berkshire Regiment (19th District).

NEW, PAUL MICHAEL (1974-87). b 30.9.1953 Wokingham. ed Woodley SS. lhb. rmf. Cap (1975). Club: Reading.

NEWBERRY, WILLIAM FREDERICK ERNEST (1908-29). Clubs: Berkshire Amateurs, Wargrave, Hurst.

NICHOLL, Major KENNETH ILTYD (1902-23). b 13.2.1885 Marylebone, London. d 2.3.1952 Famagusta, Cyprus. ed Eton; OU (Magdalen). rhb. Also Middlesex. Grandson of F.I. (CU). Clubs: Wargrave, Slough.

NICHOLSON, GEOFFREY (1900). b 5.1880 Bray, Maidenhead. d 3.5.1935 Withypool, Somerset. ed Uppingham. Club: Maidenhead.

NICHOLSON, KENNETH FLETCHER (1937-46). b 1.1.1910 Hemsworth, Yorkshire. d 21.3.1969 Birmingham, Warwickshire. ed Bootham S; CU (St John's).

NORMAN, JOHN WILLIAM (1966). b 22.8.1936 Maidstone, Kent. ed Millfield; Downside; CU (Queens'). rhb. wk. Also CU.

NORRIS, AUBREY (1930-33). b 3Q.1908 Maidenhead. Club: Berkshire Amateurs.

NORRIS, THOMAS PILKINGTON WATT (1912-29). b 2Q.1892 Reading. d 21.11.1960 St Albans, Hertfordshire. ed Rugby; OU. Clubs: Reading, Radlett.

NORTHOVER, CECIL MERVYN (1949-51). b 21.12.1912 Ipswich, Suffolk. d 10.1.2000 Cheltenham, Gloucestershire. rhb. Club: Reading.

NUNN, FREDERICK ARTHUR (1950). b 4.10.1913 Sheffield, Yorkshire. d 8.1.1978 Oxford. Cap (1950). Also Oxfordshire. Squash (Oxfordshire). Clubs: South Oxford Amateurs.

NURSE, LEE HARVEY (1997-2004). b 24.12.1976 Basingstoke, Hampshire. ed Harrier Costello S; Queen Mary SFC; Basingstoke and Luton U. Also MCCA (lo), Glamorgan II, Derbyshire II, Hampshire II, Derbyshire CB. Great-nephew of S.M. (West Indies). Club: Basingstoke.

ORTON, RICHARD FRANCIS BREFFITT (1973-76). b 31.1.1947 Lydney, Gloucestershire. ed Reading S. rhb. ob. Club: Reading.

O'SULLIVAN, MICHAEL JOSEPH (1995-2004). b 16.11.1973 Reading. ed Forest S. lhb. sla. Also MCCA (u-25), Gloucestershire II, Sussex II, Warwickshire II. Clubs: Hurst, Finchampstead, Reading.

O'TOOLE, RICHARD VINCENT (1993-95). b 12.8.1966 Leicester. ed Harry Carlton CS; Bradford U. rhb. rm. Also Nottinghamshire II. Clubs: Kidmore End, Falkland.

OWEN, RICHARD GREGORY (1982). b 19.10.1948 Mitcham, Surrey. ed Reading S. rhb. wk. Club: Old Redingensians.

OWEN, WILLIAM ALFRED (1914). b 4Q.1881 Easthampstead.

OWENS, JOHN AUSTIN (1949-50). b 16.2.1927. d 3.7.1998 Reading.

OXLEY, PHILIP JOHN (1988-95). b 7.4.1966 Reading. ed Forest GS; Bristol P. rhb. ob/rmf. Cap (1992). Also Gloucestershire II. Tours: Berkshire to New Zealand; to South Africa. Clubs: Finchampstead, Barnt Green, Wokingham.

PACKER, JOHN LINCOLN (1971). b 18.7.1937 Canterbury, Kent. lhb.rm. Club: Reading.

PAGE-ROBERTS, Captain FREDERICK WILLIAM (1909). b 4Q.1889 Depwade, Scole, Norfolk. d 7.12.1938 Lambeth, London. ed South East Agricultural C.

PAICE, CHARLES (1900). b 6.1875 Windsor. d 25.3.1931 Egham, Surrey. ed Bradfield. Club: Silwood Park.

PALMER, ERIC JOHN (1955). b 16.6.1931 Romford, Essex. ed Hylands SS, Hornchurch. lhb. rfm. Also Essex. Club: Huntley and Palmers.

PALMER, GERALD EUSTACE HOWELL (1925-30). b 9.6.1904 Newbury. d 7.2.1984 Newbury. ed Winchester; OU (New College). wk. MP Winchester (1935-45). Brother of R.H. Club: Reading Biscuit Factory.

PALMER, REGINALD HOWARD REED (1920-30). b 7.4.1898 Wokingham. d 15.2.1970 Hurstgrove, Reading. ed Eton. Clubs: Reading Biscuit Factory, Berkshire Gentlemen.

PALMER, Lt-Colonel RODNEY HOWELL (1928-29). b 24.11.1907 Sherfield-on-Loddon, Hampshire. d 24.4.1987 Newbury. ed Harrow; CU (Pembroke). rhb. rf. Also CU, Hampshire, MCCA, Egypt. Brother of G.E.H.

PARSON, ANTHONY JAMES (2006). b 28.3.1984 Reading. ed Winchester U. rhb. rfm. Club: Finchampstead.

PATEL, SAMEER SATESH (1996-2004). b 16.6.1976 Reading. ed Reading S; Birmingham U. rhb. ob. Also MCCA (ST, u-25). Tour: Berkshire to South Africa. Clubs: Reading, Barnt Green.

PATEMAN, CHARLES ROBERT (1929-34). b 5.3.1904 St Pancras, London. d 18.8.1988 Holcombe, Dawlish, Devon. ed Reading U. wk. Cap (1933). Club: Huntley and Palmers.

PAVEY, JOHN MICHAEL (1956-57). b 3Q.1939 Exeter, Devon. ed Wellington. rhb. Also Canada. Rugby (Canada). Club: Wellington College.

PEACH, HERBERT ALAN (1932-34). b 6.10.1890 Maidstone, Kent. d 8.10.1961 North End, Newbury. rhb. rm. Cap (1933). Also Surrey (Cap 1920). Tour: Sir J Cahn's XI to Jamaica. Coach Surrey CCC. Groundsman Reading CC.

PEAKE, Rev. EDWARD (1898-1906). b 29.3.1860 Tideham, Chepstow, Monmouthshire. d 3.1.1945 Huntingdon. ed Marlborough; OU (Oriel). rhb. rf. Also OU (3), Gloucestershire,. Rugby (Wales (1), Chepstow). Club: Reading.

PECK, Major-General RICHARD LESLIE (1969-71). b 27.5.1937 Rushden, Northamptonshire. ed Wellingborough; RMA Sandhurst; Royal Military College of Science. rhb. ob. Also Combined Services, Northamptonshire II. Brother of D.A. (CU). Club: Royal Engineers.

PERKINS, JONATHAN ROY (1998-2005). b 9.10.1978 Reading. ed Moulsford PS; Bradfield; Reading U. rhb. Cap (2002). Also MCCA u-25), Surrey II. Club: Reading.

PERKINS, WILLIAM EDWIN (1966-73). b 21.12.1936 Ashford, Middlesex. lhb. ob. ed Wraysbury SM; Staines GS. Cap (1967). Hockey (South, Berkshire). Club: Maidenhead and Bray.

PHILLIPS, GEORGE ALAN (1968). b 26.5.1932 Kingston-upon-Thames, Surrey. d 10.1996 Slough, Buckinghamshire. Club: Bracknell.

PHILLIPS, JOHN (1970-71). b 30.9.1932 Reading. ed Oratory. rhb. rm. Club: Reading.

PHILLIPS, NEVADA (1978-80). b 15.1.1957 Barbados. rhb. ob. Cap (1980). Also Hampshire II. Club: Basingstoke.

PICKERING, ANTHONY DERWENT (1969-70). b 25.8.1935 Salisbury, Wiltshire. d 29.1.2003 Broadwindsor, Dorset. ed Sherborne; OU (Christ Church). rhb. Also Oxfordshire. Rugby (Oxfordshire).

PICKERING, JOHN EDWARD (1969-70). b 26.9.1936 Marylebone, London. lhb. sla.

PICKETT, FRANK CHARLES (1951-62). b 28.10.1919 Shoreditch, Middlesex. d 2.5.1988 Bedford. rhb. rfm. Cap (1952). Also Dorset. Football (Weymouth). Club: Reading.

PITCHER, NICHOLAS WILLIAM (1991-96). b 28.5.1966 Welwyn Garden City, Hertfordshire. ed Kennett S. rhb. ob. Also Hampshire II. Brother of R.J. Clubs: Falkland, Reading.

PITCHER, ROBERT JAMES (1993-95). b 29.4.1964 Welwyn Garden City, Hertfordshire. ed Kennett S. rhb. sla. Cap (1995). Brother of N.W. Club: Falkland.

PLUM, HARRY VICTOR (1896). b 2Q.1868 Worcester, Worcestershire. d 22.12.1955 Penzance, Cornwall. ed Worcester Free S; OU (Hertford). Clubs: Reading School, Reading.

PORTER, DAVID ANTHONY (1999-2000). b 18.1.1982 Reading. ed Emmbrook S. lhb. lfm. Club: Finchampstead.

PORTMAN, FRANCIS JOHN (1896). b 24.3.1878 Corton Denham, Somerset. d 2.5.1905 Ajmer, India. ed Radley; OU (Christ Church). rhb. rfm. Also Somerset, Punjab. Nephew of O.Mordaunt (MCC). Club: Radley College.

POTT, JOHN ARTHUR (1898). b 17.11.1865 Highgate, London. d 13.3.1920, Ross-on-Wye, Herefordshire. ed Haileybury; OU (Keble). Also Oxfordshire. Club: Reading.

POTTER, CHRISTOPHER MICHAEL ST GEORGE (1964-74). b 28.3.1947 Reading. ed Wellington; London U; CU (Trinity). rhb. ob. Brother of S.H.A. and T.N.B. Club: Eversley.

POTTER, SIMON HUGH ARNOLD (1969). b 4Q.1949 Reading. ed Wellington. rhb. ob. Brother of C.M.S. and T.N.B. Club: Eversley.

POTTER, TIMOTHY NIGEL BARNARD (1970). b 15.1.1952 Reading. ed Wellington. Brother of C.M.S. and S.H.A. Club: Eversley.

PRICE, FREDERICK STUART (1950-52). b 22.2.1932 Reading. ed Reading S; Oundle; OU (St John's). rhb. Club: Berkshire Gentlemen.

PRICHARD, PAUL JOHN (2002-05). b 7.1.1965 Billericay, Essex. ed Brentwood CHS. rhb. rm. Cap (2002). Also Essex (Captain 1995-98, Cap 1986), England YC. Tour: England A to Australia. Club: Avorians.

PULLEY, NORMAN (1932). b 1Q.1903 Aston, Warwickshire. Also Worcestershire II.

PULLIN, JOHN DAVID (1973). b 11.10.1944 Old Windsor. rhb. lb. Club: Windsor and Eton.

RADFORD, TOBY ALEXANDER (1998-99). b 3.12.1971 Caerphilly, Glamorgan. ed St Bartholomew's S, Newbury; City U, London. rhb. ob. Also Middlesex, Sussex, Hampshire II, Glamorgan II, Northamptonshire II, Hampshire CB, NAYC. Tours: England u-19 to Australia; to New Zealand. Club: Hungerford.

RAMSDEN, ARTHUR DOBSON (1946-49). b 19.12.1913 Hunslet, Yorkshire. d 9.6.1993 Eastwood, Southend, Essex. lhb. Cap (1952). Also Northumberland. Club: Reading.

REA, LESLIE WALTER (otherwise Walter Leslie) (1947). b 31.5.1920 Gloucester. d 20.9.2004 Alfold, Cranleigh, Surrey.

RELF, ALBERT EDWARD (1895-97). b 26.6.1874 Burwash, Sussex. d 26.3.1937 Wellington College, Crowthorne. rhb. ob. Also England (13), Sussex, London County, Auckland, Norfolk. Tours: MCC to Australia; to South Africa; to West Indies. Brother of E.H. (Sussex) and R.R. Professional Wellington College. Club: Finchampstead.

RELF, ROBERT RICHARD (1900-46) b 1.9.1883 Sandhurst. d 28.4.1965 Reading. rhb. rfm. Also Sussex, MCCA (fc,sc). Tour: MCC to South Africa. Brother of A.E. and E.H. (Sussex). Coach Charterhouse S; Westminster S; Northumberland House S; Leighton Park S. Club: Reading.

REMNANT, Hon. PETER FARQUHARSON (1920-38). b 21.9.1897 Paddington, London. d 31.1.1968 Oxford. ed Eton; OU (Magdalen). rhb. Also MCCA (fc). MP for Wokingham (1950-59). Brother of R.J.F., nephew of R.C.Gosling (Essex). Clubs: Berkshire Gentlemen, Wargrave.

REMNANT, Hon. ROBERT JOHN FARQUHARSON (in 1933 became 2nd Baron Remnant) (1920-36). b 29.3.1895 Westminster, London. d 4.6.1967 Bear Place, Twyford. ed Eton; OU (Magdalen). rhb. rmf. Also MCCA (fc). Brother of P.F., nephew of R.C.Gosling (Essex). Club: Wargrave.

REVILL, ALAN CHAMBERS (1963-68). b 27.3.1923 Sheffield, Yorkshire. d 6.7.1998 Brent, London. rhb. ob. Cap (1963). Also Derbyshire (Cap 1947), Leicestershire (Cap 1958). Tour: Surridge XI to Bermuda. Son of T.F. (Derbyshire). Club: Reading.

RHODES, CECIL (1948). b 12.8.1906 Preston, Lancashire. d 11.2.1980 New York, United States of America. lhb. sla. Also Lancashire.

RICHARDSON, MICHAEL KENNETH (1975-82). b 5.3.1946 Rotherham, Yorkshire. lhb. rm. Clubs: Basingstoke, Newbury.

RIDLEY, ROBERT MICHAEL (1972-73). b 8.1.1947 Oxford. ed Clifton; OU (St Edmund Hall). rhb. rm. Also OU (3), Ireland, Gloucestershire II.

ROAST, CHARLES BARRYMORE (1972-74). b 9.1.1942 Abadan, Iran. ed St Paul's. rhb. lb.

ROBERTS, MICHAEL DAVID TUDOR (2006). b 13.3.1989 Oxford. ed Oratory S. rhb. ob. Also Middlesex II. Club: Henley.

ROBERTS, THEOPILE EDDISON (1984-85). b 23.1.1959 Antigua, West Indies. rhb. rfm. Club: Highgate.

ROBEY, CECIL JOHN (1938). b 2.5.1911 Slough. d 24.12.1993 High Wycombe, Buckinghamshire. lhb. wk. Also Buckinghamshire. Father of D.A. Club: Slough.

ROBEY, DAVID ARTHUR (1973). b 10.2.1943 Slough, Buckinghamshire. ed Abingdon S. rhb. rm. Son of C.J. Club: Finchampstead.

ROBINSON, ALBERT GEORGE (1951-55). b 22.3.1917 Leicester. ed Wyggeston GS. rhb. rfm. Cap (1951). Also Northamptonshire, Cambridgeshire. Coach Radley School.

ROLLINS, ANDERSON (1982-84). b 5.9.1951 Barbados, West Indies. rhb. rfm. Clubs: Associated Biscuits, Purley.

ROOPE, GRAHAM RICHARD JAMES (1963-88). b 12.7.1946 Fareham, Hampshire. d 26.11.2006 St Georges, Grenada, West Indies. ed Bradfield. rhb. rm. Cap (1983). Also England (21), Surrey (Cap 1969), Griqualand West, MCCA (fc,sc,BHC,odm,lo). Tours: MCC to Ceylon and Far East; to Pakistan, India and Ceylon; Robins to South Africa; England to Pakistan and New Zealand; International Wanderers to South Africa; to Rhodesia; Berkshire to Hong Kong. Football (Corinthian Casuals). Clubs: Nelson (pro), Horsham.

ROWE, Major ERNEST FENTIMAN (1907-11). b 27.1.1866 Hartford End, Essex. d 14.4.1918 Hyde Park, London. ed Felsted; CU (Clare). wk. Also Essex, Bombay, Bedfordshire. Brother of F.E., son of A.W. (CU). Club: Wokingham.

ROWE, FRANCIS ERSKINE (1900-11). b 30.11.1864 Hartford End, Essex. d 17.5.1928 Littlehampton, Sussex. ed Felsted; Marlborough; CU (Trinity). rhb. wk. Also Essex. Brother of E.F., son of A.W. (CU). Clubs: Heathlands, Wokingham.

ROWLAND, JOHN EDWARD GRAHAM (1924-30). b 3.10.1905 Reading. d 5.9.1973 St Pancras, London. ed Radley. Also Devon. Clubs: Radley College, Berkshire Amateurs.

RUDD, JOHN COOPER (1951-68). b 7.9.1932 Marylebone, London. d 15.12.1995 Kensington, London. ed Reading S. Rugby (Berkshire, Thames Valley, Wasps, English Schools). Club: Maidenhead and Bray.

RUSSELL, WILLIAM ERIC (1976-77). b 3.7.1936 Dumbarton, Scotland. ed Atholl House. rhb. rm. Also England (10), Middlesex. Tours: MCC to New Zealand; to India and Pakistan; to Australia and New Zealand. Club: Sonning.

RYLAND, Lieut-Colonel GORDON HERBERT KONCELIK (1921-26). b 3.6.1901 Windsor. ed Imperial Service College; RMC Sandhurst. Also Army. Club: RMC.

SAGHEER, KHALID MOHAMMAD (1993). d 24.1.1971 Dina, Punjab, Pakistan. ed Reading C. rhb. rm. Also Northamptonshire II, Hampshire II, Leicestershire II, Middlesex II. Club: Reading.

SALMON, ALAN GALE (1937-38). b 29.12.1919 Chorlton-cum-Hardy, Manchester, Lancashire. d 11.3.1998 Tunbridge Wells, Kent. ed Reading S. Rugby (Berkshire Public Schools). Brother of M.A. Club: Reading School.

SALMON, MICHAEL ALEXANDER (1946-62). b 9.8.1925 Reading. d 16.5.2006 Poole, Dorset. ed Reading S. rhb. Cap (1946). Brother of A.G., brother-in-law of C.D.Williams. Club: Reading.

SALTER, KEITH JOHN (1965-74). b 21.4.1940 Middlesex. d 11.4.1983 Rookley, Isle of Wight. rhb. rm. Cap (1971). Also Kent II. Club: Maidenhead and Bray.

SANSUM, ALFRED (1904-06). b 2Q.1881 Letcombe Regis. d 27.1.1913 Wantage.

SAUNDERS, CHRISTOPHER JOHN (1971). b 7.5.1940 West Worthing, Sussex. ed Lancing; OU (Wadham); CU (Pembroke). rhb. wk. Cap (1971). Also CU, OU. Football (OU).

SAYLES, GEORGE (1928-49). b 26.3.1899 Sheffield, Yorkshire. d 6.1971 Wokingham. Football (Reading, York). wk. Club: Sutton Seeds (pro).

SAYLES, KENNETH JOHN (1958). b 19.3.1926 Reading. d 9.2.2003 Richmond, Surrey. ed Reading S. Club: Old Redingensians.

SCHOLFIELD, JOHN ALEXANDER (1966-73). b 1947 New Zealand. ed Reading S; CU (Magdalene). rhb. sla. Cap (1967). Also Hampshire II. Club: Reading.

SCOTT, GARY (1985). b 14.3.1964 Isleworth, Middlesex. rhb. Club: Reading.

SCOTT, JOHN E. (1956-58). ed Reading U.

SEAGER, CHRISTOPHER PAUL (1970). b 5.4.1951 Marandelas, Salisbury, Rhodesia. ed Peterhouse S., Rhodesia; CU (Jesus). rhb. Also CU (1), Zimbabwe B, Zimbabwe Country Districts. Brother of M.A.J.

SEAGER, MICHAEL ANTHONY JOHN (1969-70). b 8.12.1947 Salisbury, Rhodesia. ed Reading U. lhb. rm. Also Rhodesia B, Zimbabwe Country Districts, Mashonaland Country Districts, UAU. Brother of C.P.

SEARS, LESLIE ALAN (1946-51). b 9.7.1927 Lewisham, Kent. d 19.3.2004 Reading. ed Reading S. lhb. ob. County Club Chairman (1983-2004). Cap (1947). Also Army. Father of R.A.C., son of L.D. Clubs: Richmond, Reading.

SEARS, LESLIE DANIEL (1933-35). b 12.1.1901 Wokingham. d 27.6.1992 Amesbury Abbey, Wiltshire. lhb. Also Essex. Father of L.A., grandfather of R.A.C. Clubs: Wokingham, Berkshire Gentlemen.

SEARS, RICHARD ALAN CHARLES (1978-80). b 5.8.1953 Reading. ed St Edward's S, Oxford . rhb. Also Hampshire II. Son of L.A., grandson of L.D. Clubs: Maidenhead and Bray, Reading.

SETH-SMITH, KEITH JOHN (1906-08). b 24.9.1882 Bradfield. d 30.10.1959 Kensington, London. ed Malvern; CU (Clare). Father of D.J. (Free Foresters). Clubs: Reading, Basingstoke.

SEYMOUR, JOHN (1931). b 24.8.1881 Brightling, Sussex. d 1.12.1967 Daventry, Northamptonshire. rhb. sla. Also Sussex, Northamptonshire. Brother of James (Kent).

SEYMOUR, STUART ANTHONY (1997-2001). b 3.3.1974 Ascot. ed Bradfield; Newcastle U. rhb. ob. Also MCCA (u-25). Clubs: Wokingham, Finchampstead.

SHARP, RAYMOND (1957). b 13.3.1939 Maidenhead. d 7.2001 Slough. sla. Club: Maidenhead and Bray.

SHARPE, Colonel ALFRED GERALD MEREDITH (1913-14). b 3Q.1884 Brompton, Middlesex. d 3Q.1966 Marylebone, London. ed RMC Sandhurst. Clubs: Reading, Berkshire Gentlemen.

SHAW, DAVID ANDREW (1990-95). b 10.2.1967 Maidenhead. ed Desborough S. rhb. rmf. Cap (1995). Hockey (Berkshire). Tour: Berkshire to South Africa. Clubs: Finchampstead, Boyne Hill.

SHAW, FRANCIS JOHN PARLANE (1922-23). b 1Q.1903 Chorlton-cum-Hardy, Manchester, Lancashire. d 29.10.1952 Windsor. ed Wellington. Club: Wokingham.

SHAW, STEPHEN (2000). b 21.12.1976 Maidenhead. ed Cox Green CS; Wolverhampton U. rhb. rm. Also MCCA (u-25). Club: Reading.

SHEA-SIMONDS, STEPHEN VICTOR (1898-1905). b 6.1874 Reading. d 13.5.1955 Bradfield. ed Bradfield. wk. Club: Reading.

SHERRARD, PATRICK (1946). b 7.1.1919 Mickleover, Derbyshire. d 11.1.1997 Exeter, Devon. ed Stowe; CU (Magdalene). rhb. Also CU, Leicestershire. Rugby (CU (Blue)).

SHILVOCK, DANIEL JAMES FRANCIS (2006-08). b 22.11.1983 Birmingham, Warwickshire. ed KES, Birmingham; Durham U. rhb. lb. Cap (2008). Also Herefordshire, Derbyshire II, Durham UCCE. Clubs: Falkland, Leicester Ivanhoe.

SHINE, KEVIN JAMES (1986-99). b 22.2.1969 Bracknell ed Maiden Erlegh CS. rhb. rfm. Also Hampshire, Middlesex, Somerset (Cap 1997), Derbyshire II. Club: Reading.

SHOOSMITH, HENRY WILLIAM (1907-20). b 1Q.1877 Sheffield, Yorkshire. rm. Club: Reading (pro).

SILVA, O. M. P. S. (1951).

SIMMONS, MARK LAWRENCE (1976-96). b 2.6.1955 Windsor. ed Forest GS; Keele U. lhb. sla. County Club Captain (1987-95). Cap (1978). Also Surrey II. Tours: Berkshire to New Zealand; to Hong Kong; to South Africa; British Colleges to West Indies. Rugby (Berkshire, Reading Abbey). Club: Reading.

SIMONDS, JAMES (1903). b 1Q.1850 Winchester, Hampshire. d 21.11.1905 Reading. County Club Honorary Treasurer (1896-1905). Father-in-law of D.B.Maurice. Club: Reading.

SIMPKINS, PETER ANTHONY (1958-76). b 27.11.1928 Dover, Kent. rhb. sla. Cap (1959). Club: Maidenhead and Bray.

SIMPSON (1909-10).

SLOCOCK, CHARLES EDWARD (1895). b 13.11.1868 Donnington. ed Winchester; OU (Merton). la. Son of C.S. Club: Newbury.

SLUMAN, LLOYD PETER (1984-86). b 13.2.1952 Helston, Cornwall. rhb. rmf. Also Cornwall. Club: Finchampstead.

SLY, ANTHONY JAMES (1950-56). b 2.12.1929 Basingstoke, Hampshire. ed Peter Symonds S, Winchester; Reading U. rhb. sla. Clubs: Reading, Reading U, Rickmansworth.

SMITH, ANTHONY A. (1972). b 12.2.1948 Edmonton, London. rhb. rm. Club: Newbury.

SMITH, MARTIN ALLAN (2002). b 30.11.1976 Newcastle-upon-Tyne, Northumberland. rhb. rfm. Club: Thatcham.

SMITH, PETER DAVID REES (1955-57). b 7.5.1926 Chelsea, London. ed Canford S. Hockey (Great Britain (Olympics), England, South, Surrey, Worcester).

SMITH, R. W. (1929-31).

SMITH, W. W. (1948-49). d 20.5.1992. Club: Bracknell.

SMITHSON, B. H. (1938). Groundsman Reading CC. Clubs: Reading, Huntley and Palmers.

SNASHALL, JOHN (1968-71). b 12.12.1935 Windsor. rhb. ob. Club: Windsor and Eton.

SPENCER (1906-09).

SPINK, ANDREW (1996). b 27.6.1976 Reading. ed Waingels Copse S., Woodley; Brunel U. rhb. wk. Tour: Berkshire to South Africa. Club: Finchampstead.

STAFFORD, STANLEY (1959). b 9.8.1928 Ingbirchworth, Yorkshire. ed Penistone GS. rhb. rm. Clubs: Reading, Berkshire Gentlemen.

STEAR, MARK GREGORY (1987-92). b 8.12.1958 Kensington, Middlesex. ed Orange Hill. rhb. rmf. Cap (1988). Also Surrey II, British Police. Rugby (Hertfordshire, British Police). Club: Metropolitan Police.

STEPHENS, COLIN A. (1967).

STEVENS, IAN LANCELOT JULIUS (1961). b 1942. ed Radley. rhb. ob. Also Hong Kong.

STEVENS, KEITH BRIAN HAVELOCK (1960-62). b 22.8.1942 Bombay, Maharashtra, India. ed Bradfield; OU (Worcester). rhb. Also OU, Public Schools.

STEVENS, MARK EDWARD (1985-93). b 16.3.1959 Taunton, Somerset. ed Huish GS. rhb. wk. Cap (1988). Also Devon. Tour: Berkshire to New Zealand. Club: Reading.

STEVENS, SYDNEY HERBERT (1909-23). b 1Q.1888 Reading. d 2.3.1959 Cheltenham, Gloucestershire. ed Reading S.; CU (Corpus Christi). wk. Club: Old Redingensians.

STEWART, NICHOLAS JAMES WILLIAM (1979-80). b 27.4.1952 Salisbury, Rhodesia. rhb. rfm. Also Surrey II. Tour: MCC to Bangladesh. Club: St Lawrence and Highland Court.

STOKES, DENNIS WILFRID (1928-66). b 26.1.1911 Reading. d 14.11.1998 Reading. ed; Reading S.; Wellingborough. rhb. wk. County Club Captain (1937-53). Cap (1937). Also Hampshire II, MCCA (fc, sc). Son of W.V. Clubs: Reading, Berkshire Gentlemen.

STOKES, Wing-Commander JOHN WESTLEY (1922-35). b 16.8.1904 Reading. ed Wellingborough; Reading U. Also RAF. Hockey (RAF). Club: Reading.

STOKES, MITCHELL SAM THOMAS (2005-08). b 27.3.1987 Basingstoke, Hampshire. ed Cranbourne S; Basingstoke TC. rhb. ob. Cap (2008). Also Hampshire (lo), Hampshire II, England u-19. Club: Basingstoke.

STOKES, WILFRED VICTOR (1914). b 1Q.1887 Reading. d 20.7.1964 Mapledurham, Oxfordshire. Hockey (Berkshire). Father of D.W. Club: Reading.

STONE, JAMES (1920). b 29.11.1876 Belle Vue, Southampton, Hampshire. d 15.11.1942 Maidenhead. rhb. rm. wk. Also Hampshire, Glamorgan. FC Umpire. Club: Maidenhead.

STRANG, Dr. ROBERT (1924-26). b 30.9.1901 Rainham Lodge, Hacton, Hornchurch, Essex. d 15.3.1976 Tylers Green, Buckinghamshire. ed Whitgift GS; Edinburgh U. rhb. rm. Also Scotland. Club: Theale.

STRANGE, Major ARTHUR PERCIVAL (1900-14). b 30.12.1880 Aldermaston. d 2.2.1952 Hove, Sussex. ed Charterhouse. rhb. Brother of F.G. Club: Reading.

STRANGE, Major FRANCIS GERALD (1903-04). b 28.7.1882 Aldermaston. d 17.12.1953 Hyde Park, London (in a bus accident). ed Charterhouse. Brother of A.P. Club: Aldermaston.

STREATHER, WILFRID JOSEPH (1939). b 2Q.1896 Nuneaton, Warwickshire. d 20.7.1962 Reading. ed London U. Assistant Coach Reading School. Club: Old Redingensians.

SURRIDGE, Dr. JOHN GILES (CLIVE) (1955-58). b 10.8.1935 Sutton, Surrey. ed Marlborough; OU (St John's); St Thomas Hospital. rhb. rm. Cap. Also OU. Hockey (OU (Blue), Wales).

SUTTON, OWEN PHILLIPS FOQUETT (1939-50). b 6.5.1913 Bockmer End, Buckinghamshire. d 4.2004 Wokingham. rhb. sla. Cap (1939). Club: Reading.

SWALWELL, Major REGINALD SAWDON (1925). b 25.6.1873 York. d 20.9.1930 Broomhall, Sunningdale. lhb. Also Worcestershire, Dorset, Yorkshire II.

SYLVESTER, JAMIE PETER JOHN (1997). b 31.7.1971 Cardiff, Glamorgan. ed Barry CS. rhb. ob. Also MCCA (ST), Wales, Herefordshire, Glamorgan II, Gloucestershire II, Worcestershire II. Club: Boyne Hill.

TATE, GEORGE VERNON (1908-09). b 21.4.1890 Kingston-upon-Thames, Surrey. d 30.9.1955 Charing Cross, London. ed Winchester; OU (Trinity).

TAYLER, GEORGE OSBORNE (1924). b 4Q.1886 Aldsworth, Gloucestershire. d 14.2.1970 Cirencester, Gloucestershire. ed Burford GS. Club: Aldermaston.

TAYLOR, ALEC THOMAS WILLIAM (1939). b 1.10.1919 Windlesham, Surrey. d 10.11.1994 Mansfield, Nottinghamshire. ed Uppingham, CU (Clare). wk. Cap (1939). Eton Fives (CU (Blue)).

TAYLOR, DAVID KENNETH (2004). b 17.12.1974 Oxford. ed Gosford H; lhb. lmf. Also Worcestershire, Derbyshire, MCCA (odm), Oxfordshire, Buckinghamshire (lo), Gloucestershire II, Surrey II, Hampshire II, Middlesex II, NAYC. Club: Henley.

TEBBS, REGINALD KEARSLEY (1946). b 8.5.1908 Headingley, Yorkshire. d 31.1.1973 Athens, Greece. ed Leeds GS; CU (Selwyn). lmf. Also CU.

THACKER, KENNETH LAWRENCE (1924). b 1Q.1902 Wandsworth, Surrey. ed Brighton C. Club: Berkshire Amateurs.

THEUNISSEN, JAMES EDWARD (2001-04). b 7.12.1981 Camden, London. ed Douai S; St Bartholomew's. rhb. rfm. Also MCCA (ST), Essex II, Sussex II, Hampshire II. Club: Falkland.

THURSBY, WILLIAM PIERS (1923). b 22.10.1904 Mayfair, London. d 3.6.1977 Sandwich, Kent. ed Eton; OU (Magdalen).

TIMEWELL, JOHN ("JACK") (1937-39). b 7.12.1912 Halifax, Yorkshire. d 14.11.2003 Trentham, Staffordshire. ed Reading S. Cap (1938). Rugby (Berkshire Wanderers). Club: Reading.

TIPPLES, KEITH H. (1960). b 1Q.1936 Cambridge. ed Birmingham U. rhb. ob. Club: Reading.

TODD, Captain ALEXANDER FINDLATER (1910-13). b 20.9.1873 Lewisham, Kent. d 21.4.1915 Poperinghe, Belgium. ed Mill Hill; CU (Caius). wk. Also London County. Rugby (England, Kent, CU (Blue), Blackheath).

TODD, ALFRED SYDNEY (1900). b 2Q.1883 Englefield. d 13.1.1968 Chelsea, London. ed Reading S. wk. Club: Englefield.

TOLLERFIELD, TREVOR (1957). b 3.10.1934 Portsmouth, Hampshire. rhb. Club: Reading.

TOMLIN, RICHARD HENRY (1938-49). b 31.3.1916 Maidenhead. d 30.8.2000 Maidenhead. rm. Cap (1938). Club: Maidenhead and Bray.

TOMLINSON, STUART ANDREW (2006). b 1.2.1980 Woking, Surrey. lhb. Club: Avorians.

TORDOFF, GEORGE GERALD (1962). b 6.12.1929 Whitwood, Yorkshire. d 16.1.2008 Poulton-le-Fylde, Lancashire. ed Normanton GS; Manchester U; CU (St John's). lhb. rm. Also CU (1), Somerset (Captain 1955, Cap 1952), Combined Services, UAU. Football (CU (2)).

TOVEY, JOHN ROGER (1947-61). b 4.7.1922 High Wycombe, Buckinghamshire. ed Cranleigh. rhb. Cap (1948). Also MCCA (sc), Buckinghamshire. Hockey (Berkshire, Reading). Club: Reading.

TOWNSEND, EDWIN (1900). b 4Q.1876 Wokingham. Club: Broad Street.

TOWNSON, HOWARD JAMES (1967-74). b 26.5.1946 Reading. ed Reading S. lhb. rfm. Cap (1972). Club: Old Redingensians.

TROWER, JONATHAN (2008). b 12.6.1979 Sheffield, Yorkshire. ed Handsworth Grange S, Sheffield. rhb. Also MCCA (u-25), England u-19, Lincolnshire (Cap 2003), Essex II, Middlesex II. Club: Wickersley.

TULL, ALBERT SANCTON BLYTH (1903-05). b 9.3.1885 Thatcham. d 13.2.1954 Greenham, Newbury. ed Eton. Also MCC. Club: Newbury.

TURNER, Major CHARLES (1905). b 11.3.1862 Grindley, Nottinghamshire. d 20.5.1926 Thatcham House, Thatcham. ed Uppingham. County Club Honorary Secretary (1904-26). Also Gloucestershire. Club: Royal Berkshire Regiment.

TURNER, Brigadier MARK BULLER (1924-33). b 4Q.1906 Newbury. d 15.12.1965 Bungay, Suffolk. ed Wellington; RMA Woolwich. Club: RMA Woolwich.

TUTTY, HERBERT JAMES (1909). b 4Q.1888 Basingstoke, Hampshire. Club: King's Road.

TUTTY, JULIAN GERALD (1979). b 5.5.1957 Reading. ed Mill Hill S, Durham U. rhb. rm. Also Surrey II, Essex II. Club: Reading.

TYLER, JOHN FRANCIS HENRY (1949-51). b 9.10.1909 Staines, Middlesex. d 26.11.1994 Christchurch, Dorset. rhb. Club: Reading.

TYNDALL, Lieut-Colonel WILLIAM ERNEST MARRIOTT (1905). b 2.1875 Kensington, London. d 1.8.1916 Roehampton, Surrey. ed Bradfield; RMC Sandhurst.

UMPLEBY, ANDREW STUART (2006). b 31.10.1980 Scunthorpe, Lincolnshire. rhb. rfm. Also Buckinghamshire. Club: Avorians.

VAN DER KNAAP, RICHARD SAUNDERS (1975). b 20.4.1947 Johannesburg, Transvaal, South Africa. rhb. rm. Brother of D. (Transvaal, Lancashire). Club: Boyne Hill.

VAUGHAN, RICHARD THOMAS (1928-30). b 28.5.1908 Mazatlan, Mexico. d 1.4.1966 Woodborough, Wiltshire. ed Repton; CU (Clare). rhb. wk. Also CU, Wiltshire.

VENABLES, MICHAEL H. (1959). ed OU (Pembroke). Also Oxfordshire.

WADDLETON, MARK ANDREW (1989). b 23.5.1965 Aldershot, Hampshire. ed Courtmoor, Fleet; Farnborough TC. rhb. wk. Also Hampshire u-19. Tour: Berkshire to New Zealand. Club: Finchampstead.

WAGHORN, DOUGLAS HENRY (1955-66). b 19.12.1929 Grays, Essex. ed Trowbridge Boys HS; C of St Mark and St John, Chelsea. rhb. wk. Also Wiltshire (u-19). Clubs: Abingdon, Reading.

WAINWRIGHT, Brigadier VICTOR LAWRENCE MOIRA (1938-47). b 1911. d 3.6.1986. ed Newton C, Devon; RMC Sandhurst. Cap. Also North West Frontier Province (India).

WAITES, Commander (RN) GERALD WILLIAM SYDNEY (1947-50). b 2.3.1908 Wandsworth, Surrey. d 20.7.1997 Wandsworth, Surrey. Cap (1947). Also Straits Settlement. Clubs: Newbury, Cross Arrows.

WALDER, ALAN DAVID (1984). b 11.1.1954 Cuckfield, Sussex. lhb. Club: Reading.

WALKER, DESMOND FRANCIS GEORGE (1947-48). b 16.3.1918 Basford, Nottinghamshire. d 22.4.1971 Pangbourne. ed Magdalen College S; Carre S; OU (St Peter's Hall). Also Lincolnshire. Hockey (OU (Blue)). Brother of G.W.G. (Lincolnshire).

WALTON, ARTHUR CHRISTOPHER (1951-56). b 26.9.1933 Georgetown, Demerara, British Guiana. d 2.2.2006 Mollymoor, New South Wales, Australia. ed Radley; OU (Lincoln). Also OU (3, Captain 1957), Middlesex (Cap 1957), MCCA (sc), Combined Services, Royal Navy.

WATERS, NICHOLAS JOHN (1988). b 29.5.1966 Clevedon, Somerset. ed Taunton S. rhb. lb. Also Somerset II. Club: Finchampstead.

WATSON, MICHAEL DIGBY (1936). b 20.9.1918 Dalhousie, India. d 22.1.2001 Chinnor, Oxfordshire. ed Harrow; OU (Balliol).

WATTS, ERNEST (ARTHUR) (1896-1908). b 19.3.1872 Woolhampton, Newbury. wk. Football (Reading, Notts County, West Ham United, New Brompton, Clapton Orient). Professional.

WATTS, PETER WILLETT (1964-78). b 17.7.1947 Penang, Malaya. ed Bradfield. sla. Also MCC Young Amateurs, Public Schools, Southern Schools. Tour: England Schools to South Africa. Club: Reading.

WEBB, Corporal (1904).

WELLS, HENRY DOUGLAS (1896-1910). b 2Q.1875 Newbury. Club: Newbury.

WEST, CHRISTOPHER (1984). b 1.8.1966 Walthamstow, Essex. rhb. sla. Club: Reading.

WEST, PETER J. (1966-70). b 1Q.1935 Windsor. rhb. Club: Maidenhead and Bray.

WETHERED, Brigadier HERBERT LAURENCE (1897-99). b 10.1878 Cookham. d 2.1.1953 Hillingdon, Middlesex. ed Radley; RMC Sandhurst. Club: East Lancashire Regiment.

WHEBLE, GERALD JOSEPH (1903). b 28.6.1869 Woodley. d 18.3.1943 Leamington Spa, Warwickshire. Brother of J.W.S.

WHEBLE, Captain JAMES WILLIAM ST LAWRENCE (1897-1899). b 29.1.1853 Woodley. ed RMA Woolwich. County Club Honorary Secretary (1902-03). Brother of G.J. Club: Royal Artillery.

WHEELER, EDWARD JOHN (1947). b 26.1.1911 Easthampstead. d 2.8.1986 Havant, Hampshire. Also Hampshire II. Club: West Reading.

WHICHELOW, HAROLD VICTOR (1908-12). b 4Q.1889 Reading. d 14.1.1913 Reading. Professional Reading School.

WHITCOMBE, Major-General PHILIP SIDNEY (1925-33). b 3.10.1893 Windsor. d 9.8.1989 Hindhead, Surrey. ed Winchester. rhb. rfm. Also Essex, Europeans in India, Army. Brother of H.M. (Essex), father of P.A. (Middlesex). Club: Berkshire Gentlemen.

WHITEHOUSE, PETER MICHAEL WILLIAM (1935). b 27.4.1917 Birchington, Kent. d 19.11.1943 Torino Di Sangro, Chieti, Italy. ed Marlborough; OU (New). rhb. rm. Also OU, Kent. Hockey (Blue). Raquets (OU (Blue), Amateur Doubles Champion).

WHITELEY, ALBERT MORTON (1921-28). b 9.2.1901 Bramley, Yorkshire. d 12.11.1976 Beaumaris, Gwynedd. ed St John's S, Leatherhead; CU (Caius). Son of A. (Suffolk).

WICKENS, EVELYN JOHN (1902). b 2Q.1881 St Pancras, London. d 11.4.1924 Moussy le Neuf, Seine-et-Marne, France. ed OU (Christ Church). Stepson of W.O.Nares.

WIGNALL, WILLIAM HAROLD (1946). b 24.12.1908 Harrow, Middlesex. d 1.6.1982 Northwick Park, Harrow, Middlesex. rhb. ra. Also Middlesex, Dorset, MCC Groundstaff. Father of E.W.E. (Gloucestershire). Professional.

WILKINS, EDWARD F. (1957-58). b 5.6.1936 Wallingford. ed St Birinus S. rhb. rmf. Club: Huntley and Palmers.

WILKINSON, LANCELOT GEORGE WILLIAM (1902). b 3Q.1878 Wolverton, Buckinghamshire. d 31.12.1959 Moffat, Dumfriesshire. Clubs: Reading, Henley.

WILLCOCKS, Major HAROLD FRANCIS (1908-13). b 7.1890 Kensington, London. d 7.5.1919 Woolwich, Kent. ed Radley; RMA Woolwich.

WILLETT, EGBERT KNOWLDEN (1897). b 3Q.1869 Saffron Walden, Essex. d 10.1.1957 Eccleston, Chester, Cheshire. Club: Windsor Home Park

WILLIAMS, CHARLES DEREK (1949). b 24.11.1924 Cardiff, Glamorgan. ed Canton HS; Cardiff TC; OU. rhb. rm. Also OU, Glamorgan. Rugby (Wales (2), Berkshire, OU (1), Penarth, Cardiff, Neath). Boxing (OU (Blue)). Brother-in-law of M.A.Salmon. Club: Reading.

WILLIAMS, DANIEL MARK (2001-03). b 23.12.1981 Newbury. ed Park House; Loughborough U. rhb. rm. Brother-in-law of M.A.Salmon. Clubs: Hungerford, Reading.

WILLIAMS, DENNIS STANLEY (1958). b 15.11.1936 Sutton, Surrey. rhb. lm. ed Ottershaw S.; RMA Sandhurst. Also Combined Services, Army.

WILLIAMS, GEORGE ERNEST (1908-09). b 1Q.1880 Aldershot, Hampshire. Club: Reading.

WILLIAMS, RALPH AUGUSTIN (1897-1904). b 2.2.1879 Caversham, Reading. d 1.12.1958 Earley, Reading. ed Winchester; OU (University). rhb. rm. Also OU (2), MCCA (sc), Buckinghamshire, Oxfordshire.

WILTON, NICHOLAS JAMES (2002). b 23.9.1978 Pembury, Kent. ed Beacon Community C.; City of Westminster C. rhb. wk. Cap (2002). Also Sussex, MCCA (ST,odm), Sussex CB, England u-19, MCC YC. Tour: England u-19 to South Africa. Club: Hungerford.

WINTER, ALFRED ERNEST (1927). b 1Q.1894 Long Wittenham. wk. Club: Abingdon.

WITHERS, PETER JOHN (1957-58). ed CU (Selwyn). rhb. rfm. Also Cambridgeshire (od). Club: Reading.

WOLLOCOMBE, Major PATRICK AMBROSE STAFFORD (1948-49). b 27.2.1929 Dewsbury, Yorkshire. ed Wellington; RMA Sandhurst. rhb. lb. Also Army. Brother of R.H. Clubs: I Zingari, Frogs.

WOLLOCOMBE, RICHARD HENRY (1950). b 12.1.1926 Pachmarhi, India. d 7.6.2002 Bath, Somerset. ed Wellington; OU (Worcester); Edinburgh U. Also OU. Brother of P.A.S.

WOLTON, ALBERT VICTOR GEORGE (1939). b 12.6.1919 Maidenhead. d 9.9.1990 Solihull, Warwickshire. ed Holyport. Cap (1939). Also Warwickshire. Club: Bray.

WOOD, JULIAN ROSS (1994-2006). b 21.11.1968 Winchester, Hampshire. ed Leighton Park S. lhb. rm. County Club Captain (2001-06). Cap (1995). Also Hampshire, MCCA (ST,odm,lo), Worcestershire II, ESCA, MCCYC., NAYC. Tour: Berkshire to South Africa. Son of R. (FC Umpire). Clubs: Hungerford, Falkland, Thatcham.

WOODBURN, Dr. WILLIAM YOUNG (1910-37). b 27.11.1877 Dunkeld, Victoria, Australia. d 13.11.1945 Southsea, Hampshire. ed Melbourne U; Edinburgh U. lhb. rsm. County Club Captain (1920-32 and 1934-36). Clubs: Berkshire Amateurs, Berkshire Gentlemen, Theale.

WOODROFFE, ADRIAN J. (1969-70). b 3.10.1948 Taplow, Buckinghamshire. rhb. Club: Maidenhead and Bray.

WOODWARD, SAMUEL JAMES (2008). b 26.9.1984 Carshalton, Surrey. ed Whitgift. rhb. Also Surrey II, Surrey CB. Club: Banstead.

WOOLHEAD, JOHN ANDREW (1980-87). b 14.1.1961 Wokingham. rhb. ob. Tour: Berkshire to Hong Kong. Clubs: Wokingham, Richmond.

WOOLLETT, ANTHONY FRANK (1958). b 20.9.1927 Lambeth. London. d 26.1.2004 Wokingham. lhb. Also Kent. Club: Wokingham.

WOOLLEY, ALBERT WALTER (1933-34). b 2.7.1901 Wallingford. d 8.1988 Wallingford. Cap (1933). Hockey (England, South, Sussex, Surrey). Club: Wallingford.

WORSLEY, HAROLD MONTAGU (later HERMON-WORSLEY) (1899-1900). b 2Q.1881 Evenly, Northamptonshire. d 24.4.1956 Henley-on-Thames, Oxfordshire. ed Radley; OU (Magdalen). Club: Radley College.

WORT, JAMES (1946). b 24.4.1913 Salisbury, Wiltshire. d 18.3.2003 Crowthorne. ed Eastbourne C.; CU (St Catharine's). rhb. lb. Also Wiltshire. Club: Wokingham.

WRIGHT, CHRISTOPHER FREDERICK (2003). b 7.11.1971 Dartford, Kent. rhb. wk. Club: Thatcham.

WRIGHT, WALTER SHOOTER (1904). (birth registered as Walter Shooter) b 29.2.1856 Sutton-in-Ashfield, Nottinghamshire. d 22.3.1940 Leigh, Lancashire. rhb. lfm. Also Nottinghamshire, Kent (Cap 1888), FC Umpire. Nephew of T.Shooter (Nottinghamshire).

WYATT, JOHN F. (1964-65). b 16.9.1946 Oxford, Oxfordshire. ed City of Oxford GS. lhb. Father of S.J. Club: Newbury.

WYATT, STEPHEN JOHN (2001-02). b 10.3.1971 Newbury. ed St Bartholomew's GS; Portsmouth U. lhb. Son of J.F. Club: Hungerford.

WYNYARD, CLINTON TOWNLEY (1912). b 4Q.1889 Sandhurst. d 1Q.1913 Easthampstead.

YATES, Colonel JAMES AINSWORTH (1900). b 24.11.1883 Trinnilgerry, India. d 1.12.1929 Maymyo, Burma. ed Reading S. Also Europeans in India. Son of H.T.S. (Cheshire), nephew of J.M. (CU).

YOUNG, DOUGLAS EDMUND (1953-59). b 17.5.1917 Wandsworth, London. d 27.12.1995 Exeter, Devon. ed King's College S, Wimbledon; OU (Brasennose). rhb. lbg. Cap (1953). Also OU (1), Surrey II.

YOUNG (1900). Club: Reading (pro).

The following played in limited overs cup matches only:

ADAMS, JAMES CLIVE (2003). b 9.1.1968 Port Maria, St Mary, Jamaica. ed Jamaica C, Kingston. lhb. sla. Also West Indies (54), Jamaica, Nottinghamshire, Free State, Wiltshire (lo).

BARNETT, ALEXANDER ANTHONY (1996). b 11.9.1970 Malaga, Spain. ed: William Ellis S. rhb. sla. Also Middlesex, Lancashire, Surrey (lo), EYC. Tour: England u-19 to Australia. Brother of M.S. (Middlesex II), great-nephew of C.J. (England, Gloucestershire).

HARVEY, MARK EDWARD (2001). b 26.6.1974 Burnley, Lancashire. ed: Habergham HS; Loughborough U. rhb. lb. Also Lancashire, Combined Universities, Worcester II, England u-19, NAYC. Brother of J.D. (Hertfordshire). Club: Burnley.

HENDERSON, TYRON (2002-03). b 1.8.1974 Durban, Natal, South Africa. ed Durban HS. rhb. rfm. Also South Africa (20/20), Kent, Boland, Border, Warriors, Lions Cape Cobras, Middlesex (lo). Great nephew of W.A. (N.E.Transvaal).

MOSS, JONATHAN (2001). b 4.5.1975 Manly, Sydney, New South Wales, Australia. ed Sydney C of E GS, Australian C of FE. rhb. rm. Also Victoria, Derbyshire (Cap 2004), Hampshire II. Club: Finchampstead.

SOZA, CHRISTOPHER RUKSHAN (1996). b 26.12.1966 Colombo, Sri Lanka. ed St Joseph's C, Colombo; London U. rhb. rm. Also Sri Lanka YC. Club: Wokingham.

STELLING, WILLIAM FREDERICK (1999). b 30.6.1969 Johannesburg, Transvaal, South Africa. ed Michael House; St Stithian's; Cape Town U. rhb. rfm. Also Netherlands, West Province, Western Province B, Boland, Boland B, Leicestershire, Hampshire II. Tour: Netherlands to Canada. Club: Rawtenstall (pro).

TILLEY, NORMAN WILLIAM (1998). b 27.1.1981 Ascot. rhb. lb. Also Buckinghamshire, MCCA (u-25).

WILLOUGHBY, CHARL MYLES (2000). b 3.12.1974 Cape Town, Cape Province, South Africa. ed Wynberg BHS; Stellenbosch U. lhb. lmf. Also South Africa (2), Boland, Boland B, Western Province-Boland, Western Province, Leicestershire (Cap 2005), Cape Cobras, Somerset (Cap 2007).

WILSON, MARTIN JOHN (2002). b 26.9.1976 Chelmsford, Essex. rhb. rm.

BERKSHIRE CAREER RECORDS 1844-1872

Name	First	Last	M	I	NO	Runs	HS	Avg	100	50	Runs	Wkts	OW	Avg	Best	5i	10m	ct	st
A.Austen-Leigh	1858	1870	11	15	2	157	39	12.07	-	-	44	2	5	22.00	3-?	-	-	6	5
A.H.Austen-Leigh	1857	1872	9	12	2	142	32	11.83	-	-	-	-	-	-	-	-	-	4	-
C.Austen-Leigh	1856	1860	11	18	3	335	72	22.33	-	2	-	-	-	-	-	-	-	4	-
C.E.Austen-Leigh	1857	1860	7	10	0	143	42	14.30	-	-	-	-	-	-	-	-	-	-	-
E.C.Austen-Leigh	1857	1872	11	17	1	434	190	27.12	1	2	452	39	25	11.58	8-63	6	1	11	-
W.Austen-Leigh	1860	1869	2	3	0	41	29	13.66	-	-	-	-	-	-	-	-	-	2	-
W.Bacon	1849		1	1	0	2	2	2.00	-	-	-	-	-	-	-	-	-	-	-
A.G.Barker	1858	1859	2	3	0	18	13	6.00	-	-	-	-	-	-	-	-	-	1	-
G.W.Barker	1856	1859	5	8	0	58	28	7.25	-	-	-	-	-	-	-	-	-	-	-
A.Beale	1858		3	5	1	76	45	19.00	-	-	-	-	8	-	5-?	1	-	1	-
Beech	1849		1	2	1	1	1*	1.00	-	-	-	-	10	-	5-?	1	-	3	-
H.W.Booth	1853	1856	2	3	0	14	8	4.66	-	-	-	-	-	-	-	-	-	-	-
R.F.Bowles	1853		1	2	0	4	4	2.00	-	-	-	-	-	-	-	-	-	-	-
D.Burrin	1857		1	2	1	12	9	12.00	-	-	-	-	6	-	4-?	-	-	-	-
T.G.Carter	1846	1849	2	4	0	33	29	8.25	-	-	-	-	-	-	-	-	-	1	-
J.Cleave	1844	1849	3	6	0	23	7	3.83	-	-	-	-	-	-	-	-	-	-	-
A.J.Coleridge	1856		1	2	0	28	21	14.00	-	-	-	-	-	-	-	-	-	-	-
C.W.Collins	1869	1870	2	3	0	28	15	9.33	-	-	62	6	-	10.33	3-17	-	-	3	-
Craigie	1860		1	1	0	3	3	3.00	-	-	-	-	-	-	-	-	-	-	-
S.Croft	1846		1	2	0	30	23	30.00	-	-	-	-	-	-	-	-	-	-	-
F.Crowder	1869		1	2	0	14	12	7.00	-	-	-	-	-	-	-	-	-	1	-
J.G.Crowdy	1869	1870	2	4	0	210	138	52.50	1	-	-	-	-	-	-	-	-	-	-
W.Dorrinton	1844		1	2	0	5	5	2.50	-	-	-	-	-	-	-	-	-	-	-
G.R.Dupuis	1856		1	2	1	28	14*	28.00	-	-	-	-	-	-	-	-	-	1	1
C.H.Everett	1853	1860	6	8	0	116	59	14.50	-	1	24	4	2	6.00	2-7	-	-	5	-
F.Everett	1858	1860	4	6	2	66	61*	16.50	-	1	13	0	2	-	2-?	-	-	2	-
F.G.Eyre	1858	1859	5	9	1	143	65	17.87	-	1	-	-	-	-	-	-	-	1	-
E.Fanning	1869		1	2	1	24	20*	24.00	-	-	8	0	-	-	-	-	-	-	-
R.A.Fitzgerald	1858	1859	3	4	0	55	48	13.75	-	-	-	-	4	-	3-?	-	-	5	-
W.A.Forbes	1846		2	2	0	0	0	0.00	-	-	-	-	5	-	4-?	-	-	-	-
G.H.Gibbs	1860		2	2	0	26	18	13.00	-	-	113	5	15	22.60	6-?	2	1	-	-
J.Gibbs	1860		1	2	0	20	17	10.00	-	-	-	-	-	-	3-43	-	-	2	-
T.Goddard	1849		1	1	0	19	19	19.00	-	-	-	-	-	-	-	-	-	-	-
W.Goodall	1846		1	1	0	12	12*	12.00	-	-	-	-	2	-	2-?	-	-	2	-
Goodchild	1844		1	2	0	3	3	1.50	-	-	-	-	-	-	-	-	-	-	-
G.L.Goodlake	1858		2	3	0	52	37	17.33	-	-	-	-	1	-	1-?	-	-	-	-
C.A.Graham	1853		1	2	0	16	11	8.00	-	-	-	-	-	-	-	-	-	-	-

Name	First	Last	M	I	NO	Runs	HS	Avg	100	50	Runs	Wkts	OW	Avg	Best	5i	10m	ct	st
G.Graham	1853		1	2	1	38	22*	38.00	-	-								3	1
W.Graham	1853		1	2	0	5	5	2.50	-	-								2	
Grantham	1849		1	2	1	1	1*	1.00	-	-								2	
J.Green	1849		1	1	0	0	0	0.00	-	-								-	
J.Harding	1849		1	1	0	12	12	12.00	-	-								-	
E.B.Haygarth	1870	1872	2	2	0	42	39	21.00	-	-								1	
J.W.Haygarth	1872	1872	2	1	0	1	1	1.00	-	-								1	
G.Hayward	1860		1	2	1	28	21	28.00	-	-								4	
W.Homewood	1860		1	1	0	0	0	0.00	-	-								-	
C.S.P.Hunter	1859		1	1	0	0	0	0.00	-	-								-	
H.L.Hunter	1869		1	2	1	6	3*	6.00	-	-								1	
H.C.Jollye	1870		1	2	0	6	5	3.00	-	-								2	
F.J.Kitson	1853		1	2	0	4	4	2.00	-	-								-	
Lawrence	1849		1	2	1	3	3*	3.00	-	-								-	
P.Lediard	1849		1	1	0	4	4	4.00	-	-								-	
A.G.Lee	1869		3	5	1	210	108	52.50	1	-								3	
F.H.Lee	1872	1872	1	1	0	6	6	6.00	-	-								1	
E.C.Leigh	1856	1859	2	2	0	35	35	17.50	-	-	-	-	3	-	3-?	-	-	-	
S.A.Leigh	1853	1860	14	21	1	771	133*	38.55	3	2	73	4	19	18.25	6-?	1	-	10	
Leigh	1860		1	1	0	11	11	11.00	-	-								1	
Letts	1853		1	2	1	1	1	1.00	-	-								-	
F.W.Lillywhite	1844	1846	2	4	1	22	11	7.33	-	-	-	-	16	-	5-?	1	-	1	
W.Martin	1860		1	1	1	3	3*	-	-	-	-	-	5	-	3-?	-	-	-	
W.Martingell	1844	1859	1	2	0	9	6	4.50	-	-	-	-	1	-	1-?	-	-	1	
F.Mason	1860		1	1	0	3	3	3.00	-	-								-	
F.Masters	1849		1	1	1	1	1*	-	-	-								-	
H.Micklem	1860		1	2	0	1	1	0.50	-	-	35	3	-	11.66	2-20	-	-	-	
L.Micklem	1870	1859	1	2	1	37	35*	37.00	-	-								-	
G.Montagu	1858		2	3	2	0	0*	0.00	-	-								1	
E.J.Morres	1859		1	1	1	12	12*	-	-	-								2	
H.R.Morres	1859	1860	2	3	0	9	6	3.00	-	-	-	-	10	-	6-?	1	-	2	
R.E.Morres	1858	1860	6	8	2	85	48*	14.16	-	-	54	1	21	54.00	5-?	2	-	6	
Newton	1857		1	2	1	4	4*	4.00	-	-								-	
W.Nicholson	1858		1	2	0	20	13	10.00	-	-								-	
G.Norsworthy	1858	1860	10	13	1	127	29	10.58	-	-	-	-	3	-	2-?	-	-	1	
H.Paine	1844	1857	5	9	0	126	57	14.00	1	-								5	
Parry	1846		1	2	0	0	0	0.00	-	-								1	
E.Paul	1849		1	1	0	33	33	33.00	-	-								-	
Pearce	1846		1	2	0	7	7	3.50	-	-								-	

Name	First	Last	M	I	NO	Runs	HS	Avg	100	50	Runs	Wkts	OW	Avg	Best	5i	10m	ct	st
A.C.Pearson	1858	-	1	2	0	0	0	0.00	-	-	-	-	-	-	-	-	-	-	-
W.Perry	1849	-	2	3	0	19	9	6.33	-	-	-	-	-	-	-	-	-	1	1
J.C.Pinniger	1857	1860	2	3	0	28	15	9.33	-	-	-	-	15	-	7-?	1	1	5	-
J.P.Pollitt	1860	-	1	2	1	21	20*	21.00	-	-	14	0	-	-	-	-	-	-	-
E.Price	1872	-	1	1	0	6	6	6.00	-	-	86	6	-	14.33	4-30	-	-	1	-
F.Price	1870	1872	2	3	2	10	8	10.00	-	-	27	1	-	27.00	1-17	-	-	1	-
J.L.Randall	1844	1856	2	3	0	0	0	0.00	-	-	-	-	-	-	-	-	-	1	-
Rayner	1849	-	1	2	0	21	11	10.50	-	-	-	-	-	-	-	-	-	1	-
H.S.Reade	1859	1860	5	7	0	155	73	22.14	-	1	185	12	7	15.41	7-112	3	1	1	-
W.Rhodes	1844	1846	2	4	0	36	14	9.00	-	-	-	-	1	-	1-?	-	-	-	-
A.L.Ricardo	1860	-	1	1	0	0	0	0.00	-	-	-	-	-	-	-	-	-	-	-
A.E.Robinson	1856	-	1	1	0	3	3	3.00	-	-	-	-	-	-	-	-	-	-	-
C.Rogers	1859	-	1	2	0	24	19	12.00	-	-	11	0	-	-	-	-	-	-	-
H.Royston	1849	-	1	2	0	8	4	4.00	-	-	-	-	6	-	6-?	1	-	2	-
H.Sampson	1844	-	1	2	0	14	10	7.00	-	-	-	-	-	-	-	-	-	-	-
H.J.Simonds	1844	-	1	2	1	6	6*	6.00	-	-	-	-	-	-	-	-	-	-	-
G.F.Slade	1870	-	1	1	0	5	5	5.00	-	-	7	0	-	-	-	-	-	1	-
C.S.Slocock	1853	1859	12	18	0	92	21	5.11	-	-	55	4	27	13.75	5-?	1	-	6	-
S.Slocock	1859	-	1	2	0	6	6	3.00	-	-	-	-	-	-	-	-	-	-	-
Smith	1849	-	1	1	0	8	8	8.00	-	-	-	-	-	-	-	-	-	2	-
J.S.Smith	1859	-	1	1	1	2	2*	-	-	-	-	-	-	-	-	-	-	-	-
C.Stephens	1858	-	1	1	0	2	2	2.00	-	-	-	-	-	-	-	-	-	-	-
F.Stephens	1858	1859	4	4	0	8	5	2.00	-	-	-	-	-	-	-	-	-	1	2
Talbot	1849	-	1	1	0	2	2	2.00	-	-	-	-	2	-	2-?	-	-	-	-
A.Waller	1860	-	2	2	0	2	2	1.00	-	-	-	-	-	-	-	-	-	1	-
H.M.Walter	1869	-	1	2	0	6	6	3.00	-	-	40	0	-	-	-	-	-	1	-
J.Walter	1859	-	1	1	0	2	2	2.00	-	-	-	-	9	-	8-?	1	-	1	-
G.A.Webbe	1872	-	1	1	0	49	49	49.00	-	-	-	-	-	-	-	-	-	-	-
G.F.Wells	1859	-	1	1	0	0	0	0.00	-	-	-	-	-	-	-	-	-	-	-
F.Wetherell	1859	-	1	1	-	1	1*	-	-	-	-	-	-	-	-	-	-	-	-
A.Wild	1857	-	1	2	0	3	3	1.50	-	-	-	-	-	-	-	-	-	2	-
C.R.C.Wilde	1849	-	1	2	0	5	5	2.50	-	-	-	-	-	-	-	-	-	-	-
Williams	1849	-	1	2	0	5	5	2.50	-	-	-	-	-	-	-	-	-	1	-
Wyatt	1844	1846	2	4	0	7	5	1.75	-	-	-	-	-	-	-	-	-	-	-
G.E.Yonge	1853	1859	3	5	1	33	14	8.25	-	-	-	-	13	-	5-?	1	-	3	-

BERKSHIRE CAREER RECORDS 1895-2008

	First	Last	M	I	NO	Runs	HS	Avg	100	50	Runs	Wkts	Avg	Best	5i	10m	ct	st
V.K.Aeri	2006	–	2	3	0	44	35	14.66	–	–	145	0	–	–	–	–	2	–
W.R.J.Diaz-Albertini	1936	1938	20	28	7	150	36	7.14	–	–	831	33	25.18	5-17	1	–	14	–
A.E.Alderman	1950	–	1	1	0	17	17	17.00	–	–	20	0	–	–	–	–		–
D.P.J.Allaway	2006	–	2	3	0	117	89	39.00	–	1							2	–
J.S.Alldis	1982	–	1	0	–	–	–	–	–	–	33	0	–	–	–	–		–
J.C.R.Allen	1986	–	2	1	1	1	1*	–	–	–	88	0	–	–	–	–	1	–
R.G.Anderson	1986	–	1	2	1	44	22*	44.00	–	–	36	0	–	–	–	–	1	–
A.Applewhaite	1980	–	2	1	1	1	1*	–	–	–	85	4	21.25	4-58	–	–		–
J.D.G.Armstrong	1971	–	3	4	1	52	45	17.33	–	–							2	–
L.D.Atkinson	2002	–	10	6	0	36	25	6.00	–	–	229	4	57.25	2-28	–	–	1	–
G.M.Attenborough	1969	1970	11	19	1	223	32	12.38	–	–							1	–
H.J.Austin	1912	–	1	2	0	11	10	5.50	–	–	18	0	–	–	–	–		–
R.J.Austin	1952	–	1	1	1	28	28*	–	–	–	82	4	20.50	4-46	–	–		–
B.D.Bacon	1958	–	7	9	2	51	15*	7.28	–	–	419	10	41.90	2-29	–	–	2	–
W.G.Bailey	1913	1920	15	25	7	388	66	21.55	–	1	594	24	24.75	5-22	1	–	8	–
A.G.P.Baines	1909	–	2	4	0	42	19	10.50	–	–								–
F.C.Baines	1963	1977	53	43	19	300	30*	12.50	–	–	2979	162	18.38	7-29	7	1	25	–
K.C.Baines	1920	1925	10	13	0	198	56	15.23	–	1							5	–
A.F.Baker	1996	2000	5	3	1	13	9	6.50	–	–	181	6	30.16	4-53	–	–	1	–
H.S.Baker	1910	–	2	2	0	14	7	7.00	–	–	72	2	36.00	1-11	–	–		–
N.E.W.Baker	1934	–	2	2	0	30	18	15.00	–	–	23	0	–	–	–	–	1	1
P.A.Baker	1962	1978	40	62	12	948	76	18.96	–	4							35	–
A.G.Bampton	1964	1975	22	40	5	718	51*	20.51	–	2							17	–
H.Barber	1896	–	1	2	0	19	17	9.50	–	–								–
J.Barber	2007	–	1	2	0	16	8	8.00	–	–							3	–
A.G.Barker	1922	–	5	6	2	66	23	16.50	–	–							3	–
W.Barker	1895	1908	96	150	51	1222	69*	12.34	–	3	8247	418	19.72	7-35	33	4	44	–
F.J.Barmby	1900	1909	2	4	1	10	7	3.33	–	–								–
D.E.Barnes	2007	2008	11	18	3	565	123*	37.66	2	1	41	1	41.00	1-37	–	–	7	–
J.D.K.Barnes	1959	–	3	5	0	116	46	23.20	–	–								–
C.P.Barr	1936	–	4	7	0	58	24	8.28	–	–	2	0	–	–	–	–	1	–
A.T.Barrett	1970	1970	4	5	0	37	15	7.40	–	–	91	2	45.50	2-5	–	–	5	–
H.Barrett	1897	1909	70	119	9	1748	74	15.89	–	5	2465	125	19.72	9-42	8	1	40	–
P.E.Barrington	1904	1904	1	2	0	14	14	7.00	–	–								–
R.E.S.Barrington	1896	–	4	6	0	107	41	17.83	–	–	62	2	31.00	1-4	–	–	2	–
W.B.L.Barrington	1895	1896	5	8	0	72	33	9.00	–	–								–
J.K.Barrow	1990	2000	57	54	22	410	34	12.81	–	–	2919	96	30.40	4-36	–	–	14	–
A.W.Bartholomew	1904	–	2	4	1	6	5	2.00	–	–	147	4	36.75	4-100	–	–	1	–
H.A.D.Bartlett	1899	1904	2	3	1	53	32*	26.50	–	–								–
C.J.Batt	1921	1922	2	4	0	34	16	8.50	–	–	160	3	53.33	2-109	–	–		–
C.W.Battye	1997	2001	3	6	0	53	16	8.83	–	–	67	0	–	–	–	–	2	–
L.E.Beaven	2006	2007	8	11	3	97	30*	12.12	–	–	583	20	29.15	5-14	1	–	4	–

	First	Last	M	I	NO	Runs	HS	Avg	100	50	Runs	Wkts	Avg	Best	5i	10m	ct	st
D.G.Beckett	1971	1975	22	37	7	752	110*	25.06	1	3	663	28	23.67	5-39	2	-	13	-
E.A.S.M.Beckwith	1934	-	4	5	0	22	8	4.40	-	-							1	-
R.Bedding	1897	1899	6	11	3	54	21	6.75	-	-	291	3	97.00	2-39	-	-	1	-
G.Belcher	1910	1913	27	42	4	849	112*	22.34	2	2	1950	108	18.05	7-54	5	1	21	-
D.J.Bell	1970	-	1	2	1	34	23*	34.00	-	-	37	0	-	-	-	-	-	-
L.C.S.Bellamy	1950	-	1	2	0	12	7	6.00	-	-							-	-
G.G.M.Bennett	1902	1927	112	190	9	5274	154	29.13	5	31	1217	42	28.97	3-8	-	-	64	-
J.H.Bennett	1906	1908	9	17	0	263	63	15.47	-	1	17	0	-	-	-	-	7	-
F.Berry	1947	1950	22	31	6	870	94	34.80	-	8	1522	95	16.02	7-40	6	-	10	-
J.E.A.Betts	1925	-	5	7	1	94	36	15.66	-	-							1	-
H.H.C.Birch	1922	-	1	1	0	2	2	2.00	-	-	17	0	-	-	-	-		-
T.F.Bloomfield	1996	-	3	1	0	13	13	13.00	-	-	196	9	21.77	5-39	1	-	1	-
S.M.Bloyce	2003	2004	6	5	0	101	82	20.20	-	1	500	17	29.41	5-58	1	-	3	-
D.H.B.Blundell-Hollinshead-Blundell																		
C.P.Bomford	1895	1904	10	18	0	297	35	16.50	-	-	227	15	15.13	6-45	2	-	1	-
R.P.Borgnis	1938	-	5	6	0	141	73	23.50	-	1	151	7	21.57	4-25	-	-	3	-
Boyce	1931	-	5	7	1	82	30	13.66	-	-	196	15	13.06	7-46	1	-	6	-
P.N.Bradburn	1911	-	1	1	-		1*	-	-	-	31	1	31.00	1-31	-	-	2	-
P.C.Bradbury	1979	1983	18	12	6	66	18	11.00	-	-	1013	31	32.67	4-40	-	-	11	-
G.R.Bradfield	1974	-	6	11	1	151	48*	15.10	-	-							3	-
S.R.Bradfield	1910	-	1	1	0	0	0	0.00	-	-								-
T.Bradfield	1935	1937	3	4	0	11	11	2.75	-	-	181	4	45.25	2-74	-	-	2	-
R.H.Bradley	1903	-	1	2	0	3	3	1.50	-	-								-
R.A.Bramwell-Davis	1939	-	4	6	3	15	10	5.00	-	-	147	1	147.00	1-72	-	-	1	-
B.G.Brocklehurst	1933	-	1	2	0	25	21	12.50	-	-								-
W.P.Brockway	1955	-	2	4	0	105	90	26.25	-	1							3	-
J.B.Brodie	1946	-	7	11	2	152	63*	16.88	-	1	150	6	25.00	2-13	-	-		-
S.M.Brogan	1960	-	10	11	3	56	27	7.00	-	-	804	56	14.35	8-56	4	1	2	-
C.E.W.Brooks	1951	1966	99	151	29	2491	74*	20.41	-	12	2196	78	28.15	8-81	3	1	62	1
R.A.Brooks	1977	-	2	2	0	24	19	12.00	-	-							4	-
H.Brougham	1905	1913	33	57	0	1824	150	32.00	4	11	62	2	31.00	1-8	-	-	10	-
A.D.B.Brow	1955	1957	4	7	3	91	24	22.75	-	-							1	-
C.E.Brown	1900	1905	29	50	5	562	94	12.48	-	1	1031	52	19.82	9-50	3	1	18	-
L.G.Brown	1901	-	3	2	0	55	29	27.50	-	-	53	2	26.50	1-25	-	-	1	-
R.R.B.Brown	1938	1939	3	4	3	10	9	10.00	-	-	74	1	74.00	1-46	-	-	2	-
F.R.Browne	1907	-	1	2	0	14	7	7.00	-	-								-
G.A.Browning	1929	-	2	3	0	14	14	4.66	-	-							1	-
A.H.Buckham	1939	-	3	4	0	35	25	8.75	-	-							1	-
C.F.S.Buckley	1924	1935	39	48	13	464	77	13.25	-	2							59	10
J.M.Bunce	1962	1969	5	9	1	179	101*	22.37	1	-							2	-
L.A.Burgess	1896	-	2	2	1	11	10*	11.00	-	-	73	7	10.42	3-29	-	-	1	-
W.A.Burgoyne	1975	1976	12	18	7	169	28	15.36	-	-	732	43	17.02	7-40	2	1	5	-
S.Burrow	1980	1983	36	59	15	902	65*	20.50	-	3	1594	45	35.42	4-82	-	-	26	-
T.G.Burrows	2001	2003	5	6	0	92	38	15.33	-	-							17	-
K.C.Came	1956	1957	9	16	2	177	44	12.64	-	-	345	21	16.42	6-43	2	-	3	1

	First	Last	M	I	NO	Runs	HS	Avg	100	50	Runs	Wkts	Avg	Best	5i	10m	ct	st
G.F.Cameron	1924	1925	10	10	2	82	43*	10.25	-	-	52	0	-	-	-	-	7	2
P.M.Care	1926		1	2	0	1	1	0.50	-	-	8	0	-	-	-	-	-	
J.J.Carless	1957		3	6	1	49	29	9.80	-	-							2	
J.L.Carr	1926	1936	17	25	3	663	158	30.13	2	2							8	
N.H.Carter	1901		2	2	1	31	16*	31.00	-	-							-	
P.R.Carter	2001	2008	21	32	4	497	64	17.75	-	1	956	29	32.96	4-32	-	-	9	
N.D.J.Cartmel	1991	1994	19	34	13	542	78	25.80	-	3							26	11
R.G.Caryer	1928	1935	12	16	9	78	16*	11.14	-	-	620	24	25.83	5-82	2	-	6	
C.Casemore	1970	1977	28	53	8	1233	119*	27.40	1	9							16	
C.A.Caslon	1929		3	5	0	101	59	20.20	-	1	164	2	82.00	1-28	-	-	3	
A.R.Castell	1971	1973	12	8	5	53	22*	17.66	-	-	628	36	17.44	6-29	3	-	3	
J.Caudle	1938	1939	5	9	0	123	33	13.66	-	-	31	1	31.00	1-27	-	-	1	
A.D.Cave	1926		3	5	1	51	18	12.75	-	-	145	3	48.33	1-16	-	-	-	
J.D.Cave	1925	1926	5	7	1	153	85	25.50	-	1	26	0	-	-	-	-	3	
W.Cave	1899	1911	49	78	14	681	67	10.64	-	1	3554	191	18.60	7-26	15	3	36	
E.Cawston	1937	1946	21	35	2	1139	145	34.51	1	7	1094	48	22.79	8-99	4	1	12	
W.H.Chaloner	2006		1	1	0	29	29	29.00	-	-							-	
T.P.V.Chamberlain	2006		1	1	0	0	0	0.00	-	-	77	2	38.50	1-36	-	-	-	
G.H.B.Chance	1912	1913	3	6	1	45	16	9.00	-	-	191	5	38.20	3-71	-	-	4	
A.P.F.Chapman	1920	1924	27	38	3	2214	167	63.25	7	9	1128	54	20.89	7-53	3	-	46	
C.E.Chapman	1895		2	3	2	32	15	32.00	-	-	61	4	15.25	3-24	-	-	1	
F.E.Chapman	1895	1900	34	52	3	856	130	17.46	1	3	12	0	-	-	-	-	29	8
B.E.F.Cheesman	1963	1966	37	67	3	1766	120	27.59	3	8	1434	64	22.40	5-53	2	-	19	
D.Child	1971		3	5	2	76	26*	25.33	-	-							-	1
G.E.J.Child	1967	1985	174	207	61	1936	73	13.26	-	2	10	0	-	-	-	-	245	44
P.Christopherson	1897	1898	2	4	0	96	52	24.00	-	1							1	
C.F.C.Clarke	1896		3	4	0	20	9	5.00	-	-							1	
G.Clarke	1974		2	3	0	24	10	8.00	-	-							-	
J.A.Claughton	1982	1986	22	41	5	1062	79	29.50	-	7							8	
M.D.Cobham	1948		5	4	1	8	6	2.66	-	-	6	0	-	-	-	-	-	
R.T.Colgate	1929		1	2	0	69	44	34.50	-	-	207	10	20.70	4-46	-	-	2	
A.J.Collins	1997		1	1	1	49	49*	-	-	-							-	
C.J.Collins	1902	1905	5	7	0	71	33	10.14	-	-	12	0	-	-	-	-	-	
L.G.A.Collins	1895	1901	32	50	2	1300	139	27.08	1	8	69	3	23.00	2-0	-	-	31	
L.P.Collins	1897	1913	42	73	6	2118	122	31.61	4	10	630	32	19.68	5-41	1	-	18	
R.J.Collins	1908	1909	4	8	0	125	44	15.62	-	-	5	0	-	-	-	-	3	
H.L.Collmann	1899	1900	3	6	1	27	22*	5.40	-	-							-	
G.W.Cook	1967	1970	7	10	1	260	117*	28.88	1	2	11	0	-	-	-	-	6	
O.T.Cooke	1897		1	2	1	12	12*	12.00	-	-	112	2	56.00	1-29	-	-	-	
H.B.Corry	1899		1	2	1	39	25	39.00	-	-							-	
C.K.Cotton	1912		2	4	1	12	6*	4.00	-	-	93	3	31.00	3-39	-	-	-	
H.C.Cottrell	1930	1933	5	5	0	69	30	13.80	-	-	30	2	15.00	1-2	-	-	-	
M.Couzens	1972		2	0	0				-	-	116	3	38.66	2-64	-	-	-	
C.L.F.Cox	1948		2	3	0	30	14	10.00	-	-	17	1	17.00	1-13	-	-	2	
H.F.Cresswell	1930		2	3	0	15	15	5.00	-	-							1	
H.T.Crichton	1913		2	3	0	112	109	37.33	1	-	50	2	25.00	1-4	-	-	1	

	First	Last	M	I	NO	Runs	HS	Avg	100	50	Runs	Wkts	Avg	Best	5i	10m	ct	st
C.R.Crisfield	1937	1948	29	48	0	943	125	19.64	1	4	37	-	-	-	-	-	13	-
C.M.S.Crombie	1952	1958	27	36	5	433	56	13.96	-	2	105	3	35.00	1-9	-	-	11	-
H.S.Crook	1903		3	6	0	42	21	7.00									3	
A.B.Croom	1897	1920	32	54	18	220	19*	6.11			669	22	30.40	5-43	1	-	16	
A.J.W.Croom	1914	1922	12	16	2	280	46	20.00			11	0	-	-			5	
A.C.M.Croome	1895	1905	54	88	6	2076	158	25.31	3	9	2553	135	18.91	7-28	9	2	68	
C.D.Crowe	2003	2008	27	37	8	755	73	26.03		3	2913	132	22.06	8-100	12	2	21	
C.P.Crowe	2007	2008	9	12	2	286	92	28.60		2	260	8	32.50	3-58			2	
R.Cruttenden	1979		5	9	1	144	39*	36.00			258	13	19.84	3-38			1	
D.W.Cryer	1967	1974	15	21	5	131	24*	8.73			756	27	28.00	3-26			10	
A.W.Cuthbertson	1946	1954	7	10	3	75	32*	10.71			444	10	44.40	2-35			3	
A.Daffen	1896	1897	16	25	1	267	41	11.12			583	26	22.42	4-9	-		21	
R.P.Daft	1896		3	5	0	73	28	14.60			9	1	9.00	1-9	-		-	
M.Dando	1906		3	5	1	116	68*	29.00		1	133	1	133.00	1-50	-		1	
B.D.Darkin	1906		3	4	2	21	11*	10.50			57	0	-	-			-	
M.J.Dauglish	1896	1899	26	44	7	735	120	19.86	1	3							31	8
M.David	1910		1	2	0	17	16	8.50									-	
P.M.Davidge	2003		2	3	0	10	6	3.33									4	
R.J.Davies	1979		6	12	0	295	68	24.58		2							4	
A.C.J.Davis	1998		2	1	0	1	1	1.00									4	
A.T.Davis	1950	1974	179	311	28	6914	141	24.43	6	29	197	9	21.88	3-13	-		122	
C.J.D.Davis	1959		2	0	0						97	1	97.00	1-30			1	
E.T.W.Davis	1901	1904	2	3	1	17	7	8.50			23	2	11.50	1-9	-		-	
R.P.Davis	2001		6	8	0	100	24	12.50			576	36	16.00	7-95	4		6	
A.R.Day	1977	1980	16	27	4	661	78*	28.73		3	43	2	21.50	1-8	-		9	
E.C.D.de Vitre	1920	1928	23	30	8	285	32	12.95			409	12	34.08	3-15	-		26	
M.F.De Vries	1958		2	3	0	6	4	2.00									-	
R.T.Dedman	1931	1949	10	17	4	96	28	7.38			708	34	20.82	4-27	-		6	
A.H.Delmé-Radcliffe	1897		7	12	0	119	45	9.91									4	
M.C.Dempsey	1926	1932	16	28	2	561	95	21.57		3	131	1	131.00	1-25			5	
A.C.Denness	1961	1971	65	65	20	437	46*	9.71			4561	245	18.61	6-35	15	2	45	
J.E.D.Denning	1912	1913	5	9	0	232	74	25.77		2	18	-	-	-	-		1	
N.A.Denning	2000	2008	29	29	17	195	44	16.25			1927	94	20.50	8-66	7	1	14	
J.R.Digby	1955		1	2	2	9	9	4.50			43	1	43.00	1-21			2	
A.Dindar	1981	1984	28	55	3	1340	106*	25.76	2	5	87	2	43.50	2-29	-		21	
W.H.Dixon	1895		1	1	0	0	0	0.00									-	
T.P.J.Dodd	1987	1996	30	37	8	512	94	17.65		2	1455	63	23.09	5-15	2		11	
L.M.Doe	1924		2	2	1	11	9*	11.00			92	6	15.33	3-24	-		1	
H.E.Dollery	1930	1933	22	34	2	926	115	31.93	4	5							19	
J.S.Douglas	1929	1930	6	8	1	45	12	7.50			183	13	14.07	5-18	2		-	
J.H.Dowell	1896	1905	4	7	1	74	28	12.33									6	
B.L.R.Dowse	1935		3	5	0	52	20	10.40									-	
R.G.Drew	1953	1954	13	19	3	215	47*	13.43			626	22	28.45	5-34	1		10	
J.S.Drewett	1961	1965	29	48	4	1080	114	24.54	2	5							25	
B.E.Dunlop	1939		2	2	1	6	6*	6.00			51	0	-	-	-		-	

Name	First	Last	M	I	NO	Runs	HS	Avg	100	50	Runs	Wkts	Avg	Best	5i	10m	ct	st
R.E.A.Dyment	1957	1961	35	34	12	111	25	5.04	-	-	24	1	24.00	1-24	-	-	52	23
G.Eades	1895	-	1	1	0	0	0	0.00	-	-	-	-	-	-	-	-	-	-
T.J.Easby	1946	1953	5	7	3	82	25*	20.50	-	-	-	-	-	-	-	-	3	-
C.M.Edwards	1895	-	1	1	0	1	1	1.00	-	-	-	-	-	-	-	-	-	1
G.I.Edwards	1997	2001	7	8	3	44	16	8.80	-	-	207	3	69.00	1-8	-	-	3	1
H.W.Edwards	1900	1904	7	7	1	12	7	2.00	-	-	-	-	-	-	-	-	6	-
B.C.Elgood	1949	-	4	9	0	132	48	14.66	-	-	0	0	-	-	-	-	2	-
R.L.Elgood	1949	-	5	3	0	4	3	1.33	-	-	-	-	-	-	-	-	1	-
C.J.Ellison	2004	2005	3	6	0	265	97	44.16	-	3	19	1	19.00	1-4	-	-	-	-
C.D.Elphick	1899	1900	5	8	2	42	10	7.00	-	-	160	7	22.85	3-49	-	-	3	-
J.E.Emburey	2000	-	9	10	2	110	31	13.75	-	-	759	36	21.08	7-74	1	-	-	-
R.M.England	1936	1939	8	9	2	96	32*	13.71	-	-	-	-	-	-	-	-	3	3
C.B.M.English	1978	-	3	1	0	2	2	2.00	-	-	61	2	30.50	2-13	-	-	2	-
J.W.Ettridge	2003	-	1	2	0	8	7	4.00	-	-	-	-	-	-	-	-	-	-
R.G.Evans	1935	1936	8	15	2	186	42	14.30	-	-	504	28	18.00	6-51	2	-	5	-
R.J.M.Evans	1973	1974	4	6	2	34	17	8.50	-	-	-	-	-	-	-	-	3	2
A.E.Fernie	1907	-	2	4	0	47	24	11.75	-	-	23	1	23.00	1-23	-	-	1	-
H.Mockler-Ferryman	1909	1914	7	12	0	79	27	6.58	-	-	313	13	24.07	5-55	1	-	3	-
E.Field	1895	-	1	1	0	2	2	2.00	-	-	-	-	-	-	-	-	5	-
F.W.Finch	1895	1901	18	24	5	153	43	8.05	-	-	778	40	19.45	6-54	2	-	11	-
R.A.Finch	1956	1962	2	4	1	47	20*	15.66	-	-	46	4	11.50	4-35	-	-	-	-
G.J.Fitzhugh	1971	1973	13	24	5	492	90	25.89	-	3	-	-	-	-	-	-	5	-
J.H.Fitzsimons	1960	1962	8	4	3	5	4*	5.00	-	-	418	19	22.00	4-48	-	-	2	-
A.W.Flatman	1950	1958	46	46	16	173	21*	5.76	-	-	2470	114	21.66	8-49	6	2	21	-
J.E.Flower	1964	1970	37	39	9	293	55	9.76	-	1	2143	106	20.21	5-38	2	-	15	-
J.R.Ford	1955	1963	33	44	18	518	46*	19.92	-	-	1235	31	39.83	4-10	-	-	27	-
R.C.G.Fortin	1965	1970	19	29	3	791	87*	30.42	-	4	0	0	-	-	-	-	23	6
D.J.Foster	1994	1995	10	7	4	51	18	17.00	-	-	951	24	39.62	7-48	1	-	2	-
M.R.L.Foster	2006	2008	12	15	5	100	23*	10.00	-	-	-	-	-	-	-	-	26	6
R.Fox	1951	1954	23	34	3	834	97	26.90	-	8	9	3	3.00	3-9	-	-	29	2
N.K.Francis	1950	-	1	1	1	8	8*	-	-	-	26	0	-	-	-	-	-	-
T.D.Fray	1997	2006	30	47	6	1713	201*	41.78	4	6	-	-	-	-	-	-	23	1
C.H.Frith	1901	1905	6	8	1	103	25*	14.71	-	-	-	-	-	-	-	-	1	-
J.D.J.Frith	2006	-	1	2	0	35	35	17.50	-	-	22	0	-	-	-	-	-	-
E.H.Fryer	1922	1924	2	3	0	44	37	14.66	-	-	-	-	-	-	-	-	-	-
N.A.Fusedale	1990	2000	35	41	11	453	53*	15.10	-	1	2928	121	24.19	7-98	4	1	23	-
J.S.Garlick	1952	-	3	4	0	40	40	10.00	-	-	7	0	-	-	-	-	1	-
E.Garnett	1907	1910	9	14	0	757	282	54.07	2	6	283	11	25.72	4-58	-	-	8	-
J.A.Gibb	1899	1902	19	34	3	1087	122*	35.06	2	6	49	0	-	-	-	-	11	-
J.F.T.Gibbons	1958	-	2	2	1	1	1*	1.00	-	-	57	5	11.40	4-14	-	-	1	-
A.E.Gibson	1968	1969	3	5	1	6	6	1.50	-	-	187	8	23.37	5-57	1	-	-	-
D.Gibson	1976	1978	6	9	5	102	42	25.50	-	-	322	18	17.88	5-9	1	-	2	-
H.C.B.Gibson	1907	-	1	2	0	0	0	0.00	-	-	20	0	-	-	-	-	-	-

	First	Last	M	I	NO	Runs	HS	Avg	100	50	Runs	Wkts	Avg	Best	5i	10m	ct	st
M.A.Girling	1939		5	8	1	68	33*	9.71	-	-	213	2	106.50	2-58	-	-	3	
C.A.Gold	1906		1	2	0	129	112	64.50	1	-		-			-	-	6	
G.V.Goodliffe	1901	1907	10	18	2	163	30	10.18	-	-	397	16	24.81	3-9	-	-	1	
W.A.Goodworth	1961		1	0								-			-	-	37	
D.B.Gorman	1981	1988	44	78	14	1664	79	26.00	-	9	30	0	-		-	-		
J.P.Govett	1995	1996	7	9	1	120	40*	15.00	-	-	454	13	34.92	3-37	-	-	4	
C.G.Graves	1922	1924	8	13	3	72	28*	7.20	-	-		-			-	-	17	2
N.C.Gray	1980		1	2	0	13	12	6.50	-	-		-			-	-	1	
P.H.H.Gray	1911	1912	4	8	1	34	11*	4.85	-	-	123	6	20.50	2-17	-	-	1	
G.R.Greaves	1913		1	2	0	26	26	13.00	-	-	54	1	54.00	1-46	-	-		
W.M.Greenfield	1899	1905	13	24	3	324	45	15.42	-	-		-			-	-	1	
G.S.L.Gregson-Ellis	1920	1923	15	19	0	316	88	16.63	-	1	77	3	25.66	1-20	-	-	5	
D.A.Griffiths	2008		1	1	1	12	12*	-	-	-	87	6	14.50	4-72	-	-		
C.S.Guest	2008			0							58	0	-	-	-	-		
F.W.L.Gull	1908		1	1	0	0	0	0.00	-	-	11	0	-	-	-	-		
N.E.L.Gunter	2000	2007	17	25	5	516	57	25.80	-	2	1193	27	44.18	3-18	-	-	2	
A.Habib	1995	2007	13	24	4	1030	146*	51.50	3	4	99	4	24.75	2-39	-	-	9	
D.C.R.Hall	1972	1981	46	81	13	1899	73*	27.92	-	14		-			-	-	26	
H.M.Hall	1994	2000	22	37	4	800	61	24.24	-	3	303	6	50.50	1-14	-	-	14	
M.W.Hall	1975	1977	12	12	2	199	50*	19.90	-	1		-			-	-	3	
T.L.Hall	1995	2002	12	21	3	596	137*	33.11	1	1		-			-	-	3	
N.W.Harding	1934	1936	16	25	5	313	106	15.65	1	1	1184	50	23.68	7-85	2	1	8	
J.M.Hare	1923		1	1	0	13	13	13.00	-	-		-			-	-	1	
A.R.Harland	1962	1971	15	16	3	89	34	6.84	-	-	662	19	34.84	5-40	1	1	8	
H.H.M.Harris	1913		1	2	0	4	4	2.00	-	-		-			-	-		1
D.J.B.Hartley	1987	2000	65	60	9	308	26	6.03	-	-	5978	197	30.34	6-49	9	-	27	
P.Hartridge	1980		3	5	1	62	44	15.50	-	-	74	2	37.00	1-7	-	-	4	
J.F.Harvey	1978	1987	77	133	25	3235	97	29.95	-	17	142	5	28.40	3-19	-	-	43	
N.P.Harvey	1993		4	2	0	5	3	2.50	-	-		-			-	-	3	
G.M.Hawksworth	1909	1928	105	137	38	1333	56	13.46	-	3	7963	538	14.80	10-97	39	10	47	
M.A.Head	1975	1979	7	13	1	233	48	19.41	-	-		0			-	-	10	
G.T.Headley	1988	1994	30	49	5	1136	102*	25.81	2	5	896	28	32.00	4-36	-	-	10	
E.H.W.Heape	1972	1977	12	17	2	304	58	20.26	-	-	191	4	47.75	2-40	1	-	10	
T.J.Hearne	1922	1923	8	11	0	132	31	12.00	-	-	350	17	20.58	6-44	1	-	5	
W.G.Heasman	1896		2	2	0	5	3	2.50	-	-		-			-	-	1	
A.Henderson	1899	1903	22	34	1	510	73*	15.45	-	2		-			-	-	25	6
E.B.B.Henderson	1902		2	4	0	39	22	9.75	-	-	17	0	-		-	-		
J.V.Hermon	1924		1	2	0	55	45	27.50	-	-		-			-	-	1	
P.J.Heseltine	1988	1989	14	25	1	668	98*	27.83	-	4	10	0	-		-	-	4	
G.E.Hewan	1946		2	4	0	43	30	10.75	-	-		-			-	-	1	
M.J.Hewett	1981	1982	4	5	2	19	8	6.33	-	-	133	4	33.25	3-32	-	-	3	
P.D.Heyn	1981		4	6	1	206	60*	41.20	-	1	300	16	18.75	5-25	1	-	4	
C.G.Hill	1910	1913	11	18	2	452	118	28.25	1	2		-			-	-	22	
E.F.Hill	1896	1898	7	10	1	199	64	22.11	-	1	133	6	22.16	2-22	-	-	1	
A.A.Hillary	1954	1962	67	113	4	3076	164	28.22	5	13	248	7	35.42	2-18	-	-	33	

	First	Last	M	I	NO	Runs	HS	Avg	100	50	Runs	Wkts	Avg	Best	5i	10m	ct	st
M.Hinchcliffe	1982	1983	5	5	3	38	20	19.00	-	-	324	14	23.14	8-66	1	-	1	-
H.M.Hinde	1921	1932	34	41	16	103	20	4.12	-	-	2323	153	15.18	8-78	12	3	15	-
W.H.R.Hinde	1913	1914	5	10	0	58	21	5.80	-	-	-	0	-	-	-	-	5	3
J.N.P.Hinds	2006	-	1	1	0	1	1	1.00	-	-	-	-	-	-	-	-	-	-
H.J.I.Hodgkins	1911	-	1	1	0	5	5	5.00	-	-	-	-	-	-	-	-	-	-
C.P.R.Hodgson	1996	-	3	5	0	120	39	24.00	-	-	90	2	45.00	1-10	-	-	1	-
J.Hodgson	1993	1998	33	58	15	1854	101*	43.11	3	13	254	3	84.66	1-31	-	-	21	-
A.M.Holdsworth	1908	1914	3	6	0	51	16	8.50	-	-	-	-	-	-	-	-	1	-
K.M.D.Hooper	1956	1957	8	9	1	18	9	2.25	-	-	280	16	17.50	4-33	-	-	3	-
H.E.Hopcroft	1927	-	1	1	0	0	0	0.00	-	-	28	1	28.00	1-28	-	-	1	-
R.W.Horner	1994	1999	7	12	0	191	63	15.91	-	1	-	-	-	-	-	-	6	-
J.H.Hourd	1959	-	3	6	1	66	25	13.20	-	-	-	-	-	-	-	-	2	-
D.M.Housego	2006	-	2	4	1	359	170*	119.66	1	2	52	1	52.00	1-26	-	-	6	3
F.J.Howard	1905	1906	8	14	2	69	19	5.75	-	-	242	6	40.33	2-37	-	-	12	-
P.Howard	1909	1926	10	16	3	196	42	15.07	-	-	-	-	-	-	-	-	10	-
R.C.Howes	1951	-	1	-	-	-	-	-	-	-	35	0	-	-	-	-	-	-
R.W.J.Howitt	2003	2004	8	16	4	741	170*	61.75	3	3	22	0	-	-	-	-	1	-
W.O.Hubbard	1908	1909	3	5	0	43	30	8.60	-	-	119	2	59.50	1-22	-	-	-	-
H.G.C.Hubble	1935	1939	27	47	3	1176	112*	26.72	2	3	699	22	31.77	5-40	2	-	20	1
F.E.Hugonin	1935	-	1	2	0	7	4	3.50	-	-	-	-	-	-	-	-	2	-
J.H.Human	1928	1934	23	38	2	1513	231	42.02	3	10	495	26	19.03	7-24	1	-	2	-
R.H.C.Human	1926	1934	39	58	5	1597	138	30.13	1	12	1181	66	17.89	7-39	4	2	9	-
T.M.C.Hunt	1906	1910	12	20	6	221	44	15.78	-	-	1000	34	29.41	5-38	1	-	32	-
J.C.Hunter	1902	1903	6	8	0	25	11	3.12	-	-	399	18	22.16	6-25	1	-	4	-
W.E.C.Hutchings	1901	-	3	4	0	156	54	39.00	-	2	-	-	-	-	-	-	3	-
H.W.Hutson	1899	1906	21	38	1	519	57	14.02	-	2	1215	46	26.41	6-102	2	-	10	-
B.M.Huxley	1975	-	1	2	0	6	6	3.00	-	-	-	-	-	-	-	-	-	-
A.P.Igglesden	1999	-	2	1	0	16	16	16.00	-	-	103	4	25.75	2-35	-	-	4	-
C.Ingram	1949	-	2	3	0	33	24	11.00	-	-	-	-	-	-	-	-	-	-
F.M.Ingram	1896	1903	33	51	6	1021	105*	22.68	1	5	21	0	-	-	-	-	18	-
G.T.Iremonger	1955	1957	15	23	13	90	12*	9.00	-	-	2	0	2.00	-	-	-	16	4
T.W.Jack	1959	1960	9	15	0	122	26	8.13	-	-	174	7	24.85	4-41	-	-	-	-
B.S.Jackson	1989	1994	16	24	7	635	86	37.35	-	5	968	36	26.88	5-43	2	-	10	-
J.W.Jackson	1938	1946	1	2	0	6	5	3.00	-	-	-	-	-	-	-	-	-	-
K.L.T.Jackson	1938	-	2	2	0	47	32	23.50	-	-	119	5	23.80	3-72	-	-	2	-
A.E.James	1899	1900	3	6	0	96	35	16.00	-	-	16	1	16.00	1-16	-	-	2	-
R.M.James	1954	1971	62	104	10	3569	189	37.96	5	22	3573	166	21.52	7-27	8	1	39	-
T.M.H.James	1982	1986	17	20	7	323	52*	24.84	-	1	763	24	31.79	3-19	-	-	7	-
G.B.Jarrett	1966	1966	2	3	1	16	9*	8.00	-	-	62	2	31.00	2-18	-	-	2	-
W.H.Jennings	1931	1932	4	5	0	97	40	19.40	-	-	-	-	-	-	-	-	3	-
G.A.F.W.Jewell	1938	-	5	4	1	34	19	11.33	-	-	235	11	21.36	5-51	1	-	2	-
R.L.Johnson	2008	-	6	5	0	37	21	7.40	-	-	421	15	28.06	4-37	-	-	-	-
R.N.Johnson	1960	1969	20	30	5	514	85	20.56	-	1	-	-	-	-	-	-	11	-

	First	Last	M	I	NO	Runs	HS	Avg	100	50	Runs	Wkts	Avg	Best	5i	10m	ct	st
D.Johnston	1960	1980	115	191	36	4943	119*	31.89	2	32	67	1	67.00	1-0	-	-	99	-
J.H.Jones	1972	1994	161	123	53	680	33	9.71	-	1	10804	436	24.77	7-29	15	-	59	-
M.A.Jones	2006	-	3	4	0	168	70	42.00	-	1					-	-	1	-
P.Jones	1959	-	4	5	2	5	3*	1.66	-	-	248	6	41.33	2-51	-	-	5	-
C.M.S.Kaye	1961		4	6	0	44	18	7.33									2	
H.K.Kefford	1923	1924	6	9	0	147	49	16.33			157	5	31.40	3-23			1	
N.M.Kendrick	1997	1998	18	23	5	263	30*	14.61			1552	71	21.85	6-46	4		9	
H.S.C.Killick	1947		2	3	0	75	40	25.00									-	
D.C.Kingsley	1947	1948	4	6	1	17	6	3.40			91	0					3	
R.G.J.Kingsmill	1937		2	3	0	19	10	6.33									1	
S.C.Kingston	1979	1986	7	5	3	21	13*	10.50			331	11	30.09	4-28			2	
J.H.Kingstone	2004	2005	12	15	5	172	47*	17.20									18	1
G.N.G.Kirby	1954		7	9	2	120	50	17.14									6	1
T.H.Knapp	1932	1938	6	7	0	30	16	4.28			53	2	26.50	2-45			3	
G.P.Knight	1970	1982	37	68	6	1720	111	27.74	1	8	30	1	30.00	1-6			13	
P.G.Krabbe	1935	1939	14	19	0	216	47	11.36			194	6	32.33	2-25			4	
W.F.Kynaston	1909		1	2	0	1	1	0.50			48	1	48.00	1-48			2	
T.L.Lambert	1999	2008	36	42	15	468	86	17.33		1	2808	102	27.52	6-87	4		15	
P.M.Lamsdale	1995	1999	12	15	1	215	50	15.35			450	14	32.14	3-40			5	
M.G.Lane	1995	2001	56	78	27	1268	82	24.86		6	4	0					78	
G.R.Langdale	1952	1963	95	136	28	2911	99	26.95		16	5945	340	17.48	10-25	22	5	55	31
I.J.Langley	1964	1965	3	5	2	40	22	8.00			156	4	39.00	2-46			1	
S.W.Langley	1964	1973	3	4	0	38	16	19.00			109	0					2	
A.H.Larkcom	1972	1974	10	10	1	34	15	3.77			422	15	28.13	6-26	1		5	
R.K.Latchman	1980	1981	6	11	2	159	50*	17.66		1	197	9	21.88	4-36			5	
H.C.Lawrence	1952		4	4	0	18	15	4.50			24	0					1	
T.P.Lawrence	1947		6	9	0	199	83	22.11			40	1	40.00	1-40			3	
W.F.Lay	1902		1	2	0	6	6	3.00			15	0						
Leonard	1909		1	2	0	8	7	4.00			30	0						
P.E.Letts	1938	1946	3	4	0	38	27	9.50									2	
P.J.Lewington	1967	1996	151	95	42	458	24	8.64			11293	607	18.60	7-34	29	4	66	
A.H.Lewis	1931	1937	35	55	4	1031	88	20.21		6	5	0					16	
H.L.Lewis	1924	1946	110	178	11	3618	113	21.66	2	18	13	0					46	
M.G.Lickley	1981	1993	105	194	17	5861	122*	33.11	7	32	867	33	26.27	4-24			47	
P.Lincoln-Gordon	1949	1952	7	9	0	142	49	15.77			134	5	26.80	4-64			2	
D.Liston	1971	1981	12	11	3	61	18	7.62			598	20	29.90	5-51	1		3	
E.B.Lloyd	1948	1949	7	12	1	239	67	21.72		1	9	1	9.00	1-9			4	
J.H.B.Lockhart	1911	1912	13	18	5	234	59*	18.00		1	1428	82	17.41	7-86	10	3	11	
G.E.Loveday	1985	2000	134	246	18	8397	206*	36.82	13	49	45	0					109	3
H.S.Lowe	1902		3	6	0	65		10.83									3	
A.C.G.Luther	1926	1927	11	18	1	417	101	24.52	1		12	0					5	
J.C.McCarthy	1900		1	2	0	11	11	5.50									1	
W.H.McConnell	1934	1935	10	17	6	109	26	9.90			461	13	35.46	4-42			5	

Cricket club player statistics — surnames Mc–Mu.

Player	First	Last	M	I	NO	Runs	HS	Avg	100	50	Runs	Wkts	Avg	Best	5i	10m	ct	st
J.A.McDonald	1999	-	7	6	4	0	0*	0.00	-	-	592	19	31.15	5-62	1	-	-	-
P.A.Mackenzie	1947	1948	10	14	0	445	63	31.78	-	5	11	0	-	-	-	-	9	-
J.J.McLean	2008	-	4	7	0	185	122	26.42	1	-	-	-	-	-	-	-	4	-
W.R.Mclean	1929	-	1	1	0	4	4	4.00	-	-	-	-	-	-	-	-	-	-
M.D.P.Magill	1939	1976	20	31	4	388	52	14.37	-	1	76	3	25.33	2-27	-	-	13	-
A.J.Mahoney	1975	1998	23	26	2	262	38	10.91	-	1	1263	50	25.26	4-53	-	-	8	-
K.Marc	1996	-	20	2	1	1	1*	1.00	-	-	1638	45	36.40	4-85	-	-	-	-
J.D.Martin	1972	-	1	-	-	-	-	-	-	-	18	1	18.00	1-7	-	-	-	-
P.H.Martineau	1905	-	1	2	0	29	17	14.50	-	-	36	0	-	-	-	-	1	-
J.E.Mason	1905	-	1	2	0	4	3	2.00	-	-	-	-	-	-	-	-	-	-
A.Massey	1963	1988	7	10	1	159	52	17.66	-	1	44	1	44.00	1-34	-	-	1	-
S.N.C.Massey	1987	-	8	14	0	135	35	9.64	-	-	97	3	32.33	1-4	-	-	5	-
E.D.Matthews	1904	1907	3	3	1	5	4*	2.50	-	-	-	-	-	-	-	-	3	-
F.R.Matthews	1977	1979	10	6	0	116	54	19.33	-	1	592	31	19.09	5-37	1	-	5	-
J.C.G.Matthews	1904	1907	7	13	2	150	59	13.63	-	1	17	0	-	-	-	-	2	1
E.H.Maule	1934	1935	3	1	0	0	0	0.00	-	-	6	0	-	-	-	-	2	-
D.B.Maurice	1910	-	1	1	0	0	0	0.00	-	-	-	-	-	-	-	-	2	-
S.H.Maurice	1896	-	1	2	0	13	11	6.50	-	-	35	4	8.75	4-35	-	-	-	-
C.B.Maxwell	1895	-	1	1	0	14	14	14.00	-	-	10	0	-	-	-	-	-	-
J.May	1900	1956	43	64	5	1346	123	22.81	2	5	294	6	49.00	2-8	-	-	6	-
J.W.H.May	1950	-	2	2	0	20	20	10.00	-	-	-	-	-	-	-	-	1	-
P.B.H.May	1946	-	1	-	-	-	-	-	-	-	-	-	-	-	-	-	-	-
J.A.Mence	1946	1965	134	219	25	6496	182*	33.48	7	39	101	4	25.25	2-7	-	-	57	-
M.D.Mence	1961	1982	59	100	18	2062	72	25.14	-	7	2476	137	18.07	8-54	5	1	26	-
D.J.M.Mercer	1989	1994	51	94	18	3454	146*	45.44	7	19	219	3	73.00	2-36	-	-	45	-
D.Mercer	1901	-	4	7	0	125	39	17.85	-	-	136	4	34.00	3-70	-	-	2	-
P.A.Merrett	1961	-	1	1	1	5	5*	-	-	-	-	-	-	-	-	-	2	-
F.W.Metcalfe	1908	1910	11	20	2	288	57	16.00	-	-	29	3	9.66	3-10	-	-	6	-
P.T.Mills	1931	-	1	1	1	7	7*	-	-	-	25	0	-	-	-	-	-	-
S.L.Mills	1920	-	1	2	0	6	6	3.00	-	-	38	0	-	-	-	-	-	-
P.A.Mitchell	1959	-	1	2	2	0	0*	-	-	-	71	2	35.50	2-42	-	-	1	-
Mohammad Amjad	1988	-	1	2	1	10	7*	10.00	-	-	24	2	12.00	1-10	-	-	1	-
C.W.Mole	1931	1938	43	65	13	753	58	14.48	-	1	1371	55	24.92	5-39	1	-	40	-
V.R.Moon	1947	-	2	3	1	5	4*	2.50	-	-	145	6	24.16	3-34	-	-	-	-
R.D.Morbey	1946	1953	58	84	7	1510	100	19.61	1	6	3132	132	23.72	8-30	4	1	33	-
D.J.Mordaunt	1964	1974	40	74	10	2155	100	33.67	1	13	1260	63	20.00	5-35	2	1	31	-
B.H.D.Mordt	2003	2008	29	46	3	1553	111	36.11	2	9	45	0	-	-	-	-	33	2
M.N.Morgan	1950	1959	50	63	19	600	58	13.63	-	2	2568	126	20.38	6-55	5	1	19	-
P.Morgan	1971	-	5	8	2	61	26	10.16	-	-	-	-	-	-	-	-	-	-
E.R.Morres	1897	1900	7	13	0	350	83	26.92	-	3	133	6	22.16	2-13	-	-	1	-
H.F.M.Morres	1897	1923	31	52	3	1357	123	27.69	1	6	1117	55	20.30	7-50	3	-	25	-
J.C.Morris	2002	2008	20	37	2	1054	96	30.11	-	9	1024	27	37.92	5-30	1	-	23	-
E.H.Moss	1938	1939	8	7	1	281	137*	46.83	1	1	-	-	-	-	-	-	4	-
J.G.B.Moulsdale	1948	1950	8	12	0	364	109	30.33	1	1	568	46	12.34	8-32	2	1	2	-
H.J.C.Munday	1930	1931	12	15	6	108	47	12.00	-	-	55	3	18.33	2-34	-	-	8	-
A.J.Murdoch-Cozens	1911	1913	7	14	1	157	26	12.07	-	-	-	-	-	-	-	-	4	-

	First	Last	M	I	NO	Runs	HS	Avg	100	50	Runs	Wkts	Avg	Best	5i	10m	ct	st
H.E.M.Murphy	1959	1964	37	39	9	464	63	15.46	-	1	2328	105	22.17	7-46	5	-	61	19
K.S.Murray	1984	1992	26	44	5	902	95	23.12	-	4							22	
S.D.Myles	1995	2000	46	79	9	2389	122	34.12	3	13							19	
W.O.Nares	1895	1900	3	5	1	5	3	1.25	-	-	22	0	-	-	-	-		
P.G.E.Nash	1924	1930	19	30	2	397	47	14.17	-	-	683	20	34.15	5-47	1	-	18	
S.P.Naylor	2002	2008	35	54	8	2102	149	45.69	4	13	1232	35	35.20	5-57	1	-	27	
B.Neame	1927		2	4	1	73	38	24.33	-	-								
F.W.Neate	1932	1933	10	9	3	16	9*	2.66	-	-	212	8	26.50	3-34	-	-	6	
F.W.Neate	1958	1979	135	235	28	5655	140	27.31	3	28	281	7	40.14	2-4	-	-	96	
P.W.Neate	1964	1979	77	119	28	1457	71*	16.01	-	7	3109	151	20.58	6-30	4	-	45	
C.E.M.Y.Nepean	1895	1914	125	209	18	3778	75	19.78	-	13	400	14	28.57	3-27	-	-	165	
P.M.New	1974	1987	47	51	15	552	48	15.33	-	-	2613	115	22.72	6-28	6	-	7	
W.F.E.Newberry	1908	1929	4	7	2	19	8	3.80	-	-	145	3	48.33	1-30	-	-		
K.I.Nicholl	1902	1923	11	18	0	432	127	24.00	1	2							16	
G.Nicholson	1900		1	2	0	0	0	0.00	-	-							2	
K.F.Nicholson	1937	1946	3	6	0	9	5	1.50	-	-								1
J.W.Norman	1966		1	2	0	34	20	17.00	-	-							2	
A.Norris	1930	1933	9	13	2	116	22*	10.54	-	-	313	14	22.35	4-23	1	-	6	
T.P.W.Norris	1912	1929	24	41	3	768	67	20.21	-	4	191	8	23.87	5-47	1	-	9	
C.M.Northover	1949	1951	15	23	1	642	119	29.18	2	2	249	13	19.15	5-61	1	-	5	
F.A.Nunn	1950		5	6	2	77	34*	19.25	-	2							2	
L.H.Nurse	1997	2004	29	52	4	1140	108	23.75	2	5	14	0	-	-	-	-	16	
R.F.B Orton	1973	1976	14	21	3	228	52	12.66	-	1	683	22	31.04	5-41	1	-	4	
M.J.O'Sullivan	1995	2004	14	13	8	73	13*	14.60	-	-	735	22	33.40	5-59	1	-	3	
R.V.O'Toole	1993	1995	6	6	3	27	13*	9.00	-	-	198	1	198.00	1-14	-	-	2	
R.G.Owen	1982		1	1	0	6	6	6.00	-	-							3	
W.A.Owen	1914		1	1	0	1	1	1.00	-	-								
J.A.Owens	1949	1950	7	10	7	28	12	9.33	-	-	374	9	41.55	5-43	1	-	4	
P.J.Oxley	1988	1995	50	79	29	1119	63*	22.38	-	3	1261	28	45.03	3-24	-	-	24	
J.L.Packer	1971		1	1	0	4	4	4.00	-	-	43	0	-	-	-	-		
F.W.Page-Roberts	1909		2	4	2	42	31*	21.00	-	-	37	2	18.50	2-14	-	-	1	
C.Paice	1900		3	6	2	41	20	10.25	-	-							1	
E.J.Palmer	1955		1	2	0	13	9	6.50	-	-								
G.E.H.Palmer	1925	1930	12	15	2	103	18	7.92	-	-	9	0	-	-	-	-	9	
R.H.R.Palmer	1920	1930	54	78	4	1340	97	18.10	-	6	740	23	32.17	5-56	1	-	31	3
R.H.Palmer	1928	1929	11	14	4	118	21*	11.80	-	-	48	0	-	-	-	-	9	
A.J.Parson	2006		1	3	0	3	3	1.00	-	-								
S.S.Patel	1996	2004	27	37	4	512	78*	15.51	-	2	1117	36	31.02	5-29	1	-	18	
C.R.Pateman	1929	1934	7	11	3	113	25	14.12	-	-							2	
J.M.Pavey	1956	1957	7	8	0	67	26	8.37	-	-							1	
H.A.Peach	1932	1934	10	13	1	163	41	13.58	-	-	623	42	14.83	7-69	2	-	4	
E.Peake	1898	1906	7	12	3	179	47	19.88	-	-	432	9	48.00	3-44	-	1	1	
R.L.Peck	1969	1971	4	8	0	137	44	17.12	-	-							10	

Name	First	Last	M	I	NO	Runs	HS	Avg	100	50	Runs	Wkts	Avg	Best	5i	10m	ct	st
J.R.Perkins	1998	2005	22	36	3	1359	138*	38.82	2	7	12	0	-	-	-	-	15	-
W.E.Perkins	1966	1973	28	45	3	1063	79	25.30	-	10					-	-	20	-
G.A.Phillips	1968	1971	3	4	1	39	14*	13.00	-	-	393	22	17.86	3-7	-	-		-
J.Phillips	1970	1980	12	19	6	113	20*	8.69	-	-	101	3	33.66	2-69	-	-	9	-
N.Phillips	1978		14	25	1	673	73	28.04	-	5	4	0	-	-	-	-	5	-
A.D.Pickering	1969	1970	6	11	0	129	46	11.72	-	-	214	7	30.57	3-86	-	-	3	-
J.E.Pickering	1969	1970	5	7	4	30	15*	10.00	-	-	1399	49	28.55	5-25	2	-		-
F.C.Pickett	1951	1962	28	36	2	623	75*	18.32	1	3					-	-	12	-
N.W.Pitcher	1991	1996	7	12	1	344	100	31.27	1	2					-	-	4	-
R.J.Pitcher	1993	1995	10	7	5	35	18	17.50	-	-	968	38	25.47	5-91	1	-	6	-
H.V.Plum	1896		1	1	0	0	0	0.00	-	-					-	-		-
D.A.Porter	1999	2000	3	4	2	12	6*	6.00	-	-	31	1	31.00	1-17	-	-		-
F.J.Portman	1896		2	3	2	15	12	5.00	-	-	29	0	-	-	-	-	2	-
J.A.Pott	1898		1	0	0				-	-					-	-		-
C.M.S.Potter	1964	1974	8	5	3	36	16*	18.00	-	-	350	8	43.75	3-52	-	-	3	-
S.H.A.Potter	1969		1	2	0	7	7	3.50	-	-	32	1	32.00	1-17	-	-		-
T.N.B.Potter	1970		1	0					-	-	15	0	-	-	-	-		-
F.S.Price	1950	1952	10	14	0	207	46	14.78	-	-					-	-		-
P.J.Prichard	2002	2006	25	41	3	1277	114*	33.60	2	10					-	-	17	-
N.Pulley	1932		4	6	2	60	25	15.00	-	-					-	-	2	-
J.D.Pullin	1973		1	0					-	-					-	-	1	-
T.A.Radford	1998	1999	16	27	4	853	96	37.08	-	7	469	21	22.33	4-31	-	-	3	-
A.D.Ramsden	1946	1949	20	34	0	545	59	16.02	-	3	159	5	31.80	4-65	-	-	22	-
L.W.Rea	1947	1947	2	3	0	8	6	2.66	-	-	164	11	14.90	4-36	-	-	2	-
A.E.Relf	1895	1897	2	3	0	30	25	10.00	-	-					-	-	4	-
R.R.Relf	1900	1946	118	179	25	3197	136	20.75	3	11	10273	632	16.25	9-41	64	17	108	-
P.F.Remnant	1920	1938	59	84	6	1802	103	23.10	1	9	23	1	23.00	1-16	-	-	42	-
R.J.F.Remnant	1920	1936	73	109	7	3642	177	35.70	7	17	2330	123	18.94	7-34	7	-	51	-
A.C.Revill	1963	1968	23	38	6	922	102*	28.81	1	5	512	25	20.48	5-21	1	-	24	-
C.Rhodes	1948		3	3	1	1	1*	0.50	-	-	216	25	8.64	8-30	3	-	1	-
M.K.Richardson	1975	1982	22	14	7	13	5*	1.85	-	-	1103	48	22.97	7-50	2	-	10	-
R.M.Ridley	1972	1973	9	16	2	280	54	20.00	-	-	375	13	28.84	3-36	-	-	10	-
C.B.Roast	1972	1974	7	5	1	9	4	2.25	-	-					-	-	1	-
M.D.T.Roberts	2006	2006	1	2	0	2	2	1.00	-	-					-	-		-
T.E.Roberts	1984	1985	12	7	3	58	14	14.50	-	-	624	26	24.00	7-63	1	-	2	-
C.J.Robey	1938		2	1	0	0	0	0.00	-	-					-	-	1	-
D.A.Robey	1973		4	4	1	12	4*	4.00	-	-	189	9	21.00	5-39	1	-		-
A.G.Robinson	1951	1955	32	35	10	131	24*	5.24	-	-	1618	74	21.86	5-25	3	-		-
A.Rollins	1982	1984	6	9	1	132	42	16.50	-	-	383	7	54.71	3-59	-	-	8	26
G.R.J.Roope	1963	1988	55	91	25	2765	107*	41.89	1	21	1143	58	19.70	6-21	1	-	67	-
E.F.Rowe	1907	1911	35	58	7	753	66	14.76	-	4					-	-	33	3
F.E.Rowe	1900	1911	47	84	4	2019	137	25.23	1	8	258	10	25.80	4-23	-	-	38	-
J.E.G.Rowland	1924	1930	23	33	3	498	78	16.60	-	4					-	-	10	-
J.C.Rudd	1951	1968	13	19	0	330	87	17.36	-	2	36	1	36.00	1-18	-	-	4	-
W.E.Russell	1976	1977	9	17	0	417	107	24.52	1	2	29	0	-	-	-	-	7	-

	First	Last	M	I	NO	Runs	HS	Avg	100	50	Runs	Wkts	Avg	Best	5i	10m	ct	st
G.H.K.Ryland	1921	1926	16	19	2	211	33	12.41	-	-	918	46	19.95	7-60	1	-	8	-
K.M.Sagheer	1993		8	12	3	138	44	15.33	-	-	489	15	32.60	4-19	-		4	
A.G.Salmon	1937	1938	4	6	1	51	21*	10.20	-	-	148	5	29.60	2-20	-	-	6	
M.A.Salmon	1946	1962	68	109	4	2523	104	24.02	1	15							33	
K.J.Salter	1965	1974	27	47	3	696	85	15.81	-	2	17	0	-		-		8	
A.Sansum	1904	1906	5	4	1	15	7*	5.00			1021	35	29.17	5-49	1	-	3	
C.J.Saunders	1971		3	5	2	45	18*	15.00			401	18	22.27	7-42	1	-	3	
G.Sayles	1928	1949	76	121	10	1867	80	16.81		8							35	
K.J.Sayles	1958		2	3	1	29	18	14.50									-	1
J.A.Scholfield	1966	1973	31	50	6	806	59*	18.31		3	28	0					24	3
G.Scott	1985		2	4	2	74	57*	37.00		1			-		-		5	
J.E.Scott	1956	1958	8	14	2	141	52	11.75		1							5	
C.P.Seager	1970		4	6	1	59	23	11.80									2	
M.A.J.Seager	1969	1970	10	18	2	211	38	13.18									9	
L.A.Sears	1946	1951	35	51	7	475	40	10.79		1	2525	104	24.27	7-42	6	1	32	
L.D.Sears	1933	1935	13	22	0	373	70	16.95		1							20	
R.A.C.Sears	1978	1980	16	31	2	564	53	19.44		2							7	
K.J.Seth-Smith	1906	1908	7	13	2	208	58	18.90		1							2	
J.Seymour	1931		2	2	0	5	4	2.50			69	2	34.50	1-22	-		1	
S.A.Seymour	1997	2001	34	53	6	1266	102	26.93	1	7							34	
R.Sharp	1957		2	3	3	0	0*	-									2	
A.G.M.Sharpe	1913	1914	3	6	0	17	11	2.83			87	2	43.50	2-20	-		-	
D.A.Shaw	1990	1995	33	60	6	1476	132*	27.33	1	9	212	9	23.55	3-129	-		20	
F.J.P.Shaw	1922	1923	3	4	0	13	13	3.25			415	11	37.72	2-23	-		1	
S.Shaw	2000		1	2	0	1	1	0.50									1	
S.V.Shea-Simonds	1898	1905	9	17	0	349	115	20.52	1								5	
P.Sherrard	1946		1	2	0	6	6	3.00									-	
D.J.F.Shilvock	2006	2008	9	13	1	556	147	46.33	2	1	17	0	-		-		7	
K.J.Shine	1986	1999	4	3	0	31	18	10.33			202	5	40.40	2-60	-		-	
H.W.Shoosmith	1907	1920	62	109	8	2109	155	20.88	3	3	2012	53	37.96	6-34	2		89	
O.M.P.S.Silva	1951		2	2	0	29	20	14.50			141	7	20.14	4-81	-		-	
M.L.Simmons	1976	1996	148	252	45	5683	115	27.45	3	26	1061	28	37.89	4-71	-		67	
J.Simonds	1903		1	1	0	6	6	6.00									-	
P.A.Simpkins	1958	1976	121	73	38	92	8	2.62			7820	447	17.49	7-52	23	3	46	
Simpson	1909	1910	12	21	7	76	20	5.42			862	36	23.94	7-73	2		8	
C.E.Slocock	1895		1			13	13	13.00									2	
L.P.Sluman	1984	1986	18	14	2	72	23*	6.00			937	34	27.55	5-63	1		2	
A.J.Sly	1950	1956	32	32	15	117	21*	6.88			1819	80	22.73	5-41	3		17	
A.A.Smith	1972		2	2	1	7	4*	7.00			97	4	24.25	2-33	-		1	
M.A.Smith	2002		3	3	0	47	42	15.66			141	2	70.50	2-31	-		-	
P.D.R.Smith	1955	1957	3	6	0	140	50	23.33		1	584	40	14.60	7-43	4		2	
R.W.Smith	1929	1931	9	11	2	63	29*	7.00			350	17	20.58	3-26	-		7	
W.W.Smith	1948	1949	9	13	2	130	36	11.81			138	3	46.00	3-69	-		9	
B.H.Smithson	1938		3	5	1	35	18	8.75									4	
J.Snashall	1968	1971	9	15	2	156	41	12.00									3	
Spencer	1906	1909	14	26	9	154	37	9.05			663	17	39.00	4-101	-		6	

	First	Last	M	I	NO	Runs	HS	Avg	100	50	Runs	Wkts	Avg	Best	5i	10m	ct	st
A.Spink	1996		2	4	0	73	41	18.25	-	-							6	
S.Stafford	1959		1	1	0	11	11	11.00										
M.G.Stear	1987	1992	38	41	11	398	57	13.26	-	1	2424	98	24.73	6-36	2	-	21	
C.A.Stephens	1967		2	3	1	3	2*	1.50									2	
I.L.J.Stevens	1961		3	2	0	4	4	2.00										
K.B.H.Stevens	1960	1962	10	16	3	266	58	20.46	-	1							2	
M.E.Stevens	1985	1993	58	52	21	350	33	11.29									109	24
S.H.Stevens	1909	1923	22	30	3	633	83*	23.44		3							33	11
N.J.W.Stewart	1979	1980	9	12	3	87	28	9.66			713	22	32.40	4-49	-	-	1	
D.W.Stokes	1928	1966	154	234	21	5365	153*	25.18	5	24	51	1	51.00	1-7	-	-	177	77
J.W.Stokes	1922	1935	24	41	4	773	87	20.89		2	212	4	53.00	2-64	-	-	6	
M.S.T.Stokes	2005	2008	10	18	0	496	81	27.55		2	35	0	-	-			4	
W.V.Stokes	1914		1	2	1	18	11	18.00							-			
J.Stone	1920		2	4	0	66	28	16.50							-		2	1
R.Strang	1924	1926	13	16	1	134	38	8.93			315	14	22.50	4-39	-	-	10	
A.P.Strange	1900	1914	37	68	2	1059	77*	16.04		6	178	6	29.66	3-15	-		15	
F.G.Strange	1903	1904	12	22	6	168	29	10.50			10	0	-	-			3	
W.J.Streather	1939		1	1	0	0	0	0.00			69	1	69.00	1-21	-			
J.G.Surridge	1955	1958	21	36	4	761	103*	23.78	1	4	130	4	32.50	1-1	-		8	
O.P.F.Sutton	1939	1950	32	46	12	557	65	16.38		4							7	
R.S.Swalwell	1925		1	1	0	0	0	0.00			24	0						
J.P.J.Sylvester	1997		9	16	0	374	67	23.37	-	3	199	5	39.80	1-9	-	-	8	
G.V.Tate	1908	1909	3	6	1	84	28	16.80	-	-	40	0	-	-	-			
G.O.Tayler	1924		2	4	1	12	5	4.00									2	
A.T.W.Taylor	1939		6	10	0	142	81	14.20	-	1	22	1	22.00	1-7	-	-	1	
D.K.Taylor	2004		2	4	0	70	32	17.50			59	0	-	-	-		2	
R.K.Tebbs	1946		4	7	2	7	5*	1.40			268	11	24.36	4-68	-		4	
K.L.Thacker	1924		3	6	1	82	39	16.40									3	
J.E.Theunissen	2001	2004	16	20	10	86	26*	8.60	-	-	1323	43	30.76	5-28	2	1		
W.P.Thursby	1923		3	5	0	62	39	12.40									4	
J.Timewell	1937	1939	16	27	2	364	45	14.56			43	2	21.50	1-11	-			
K.H.Tipples	1960		3	3	0	15	15	5.00										
A.F.Todd	1910	1913	23	35	13	158	18*	7.18									25	21
A.S.Todd	1900		1	2	0	12	12	6.00										
T.Tollerfield	1957		1	2	0	8	5	4.00										
R.H.Tomlin	1938	1949	34	48	16	260	31*	8.12	-	-	2161	91	23.74	6-119	4	-	23	
S.A.Tomlinson	2006		3	5	1	50	25*	12.50									1	
G.G.Tordoff	1962		6	10	3	213	54*	30.42		2	94	2	47.00	1-17	-		2	
J.R.Tovey	1947	1961	23	35	2	540	60*	16.36		2							9	
E.Townsend	1900		1	2	0	6	4	3.00										
H.J.Townson	1967	1974	24	25	8	113	15*	6.64			1167	57	20.47	7-27	2	-	8	
J.Trower	2008		5	9	3	151	52*	25.16		1								
A.S.B.Tull	1903	1905	4	5	0	23	17	4.60									2	
C.Turner	1905		2	3	1	65	45	32.50			19	0	-	-			1	
M.B.Turner	1924	1933	21	34	3	513	42*	16.54	-	-							5	

Name	First	Last	M	I	NO	Runs	HS	Avg	100	50	Runs	Wkts	Avg	Best	5i	10m	ct	st
H.J.Tutty	1909		1	1	0	7	7	7.00	-	-	17	1	17.00	1-17	-	-	1	
J.G.Tutty	1979		7	14	1	342	73	26.30	-	2	3	0	-	-	-	-	1	
J.F.H.Tyler	1949	1951	4	7	0	141	73	20.14	-	1							2	
W.E.M.Tyndall	1905		1	2	0	8	8	4.00	-	-							3	
A.S.Umpleby	2006		1	1	0	17	17	17.00	-	-	36	2	18.00	2-16	-	-	-	
R.S.van der Knaap	1975		5	9	2	87	23	12.42	-	-	83	3	27.66	2-24	-	-	1	
R.T.Vaughan	1928	1930	4	7	1	75	29	12.50	-	-							7	
M.H.Venables	1959		2	2	1	3	3*	3.00	-	-							7	1
M.A.Waddleton	1989		1	1	0	22	22	22.00	-	-							1	
D.H.Waghorn	1955	1966	8	9	2	73	35	10.42	-	-	63	2	31.50	1-10	-	-	8	
V.L.M.Wainwright	1938	1947	7	10	0	166	58	16.60	-	1	168	3	56.00	1-8	-	-	2	
G.W.S.Waites	1947	1950	16	23	5	412	74	22.88	-	1							15	2
A.D.Walder	1984		3	6	2	72	30	18.00	-	-							1	
D.F.G.Walker	1947	1948	9	15	2	213	63	16.38	-	-	8	0	-	-	-	-	3	
A.C.Walton	1951	1956	21	32	1	723	134	23.32	1	5	23	0	-	-	-	-	20	
N.J.Waters	1988		2	2	0	14	10	7.00	-	-								
M.D.Watson	1936		1	4	0	9	5	2.25	-	-	7	0	-	-	-	-		
E.Watts	1896	1908	85	157	12	3450	130	23.79	2	16	747	33	22.63	5-54	1	-	98	9
P.W.Watts	1964	1978	22	24	6	148	37	8.22	-	-	47	1	47.00	1-37	-	-	9	
Webb	1904		1	2	0	1	1	0.50	-	-							1	
H.D.Wells	1896	1910	4	5	0	68	40	13.60	-	-	103	2	51.50	2-21	-	-	2	
C.West	1984		1	0	0			-			27	2	13.50	2-27	-	-	1	
P.J.West	1966	1970	16	28	3	376	57	15.04	-	1							10	
H.L.Wethered	1897	1899	3	5	0	105	70	21.00	-	-							1	
G.J.Wheble	1903		2	4	0	11	11	2.75	-	-								
J.W.S.Wheble	1897	1899	5	9	1	108	28	13.50	-	-	110	1	110.00	1-56	-	-	2	
E.J.Wheeler	1947		1	2	1	9	9*	9.00	-	-	67	2	33.50	1-33	-	-		
H.V.Whichelow	1908	1912	16	28	6	315	47*	14.31	-	-	136	3	45.33	2-61	-	-	2	
P.S.Whitcombe	1925	1933	12	17	1	243	33	15.18	-	-	379	21	18.04	5-29	1	-	11	
P.M.W.Whitehouse	1935		5	8	1	101	33	14.42	-	-	59	1	59.00	1-12	-	-	2	
A.M.Whiteley	1921	1928	4	4	1	61	26	20.33	-	-	57	1	57.00	1-28	-	-	1	
E.J.Wickens	1902		2	3	0	8	8	2.66	-	-							3	
W.H.Wignall	1946		7	13	1	156	64	13.00	-	1	390	25	15.60	4-42	-	-	7	
E.F.Wilkins	1957	1958	7	5	4	23	11*	23.00	-	-	228	7	32.57	3-38	-	-	3	
L.G.W.Wilkinson	1902		1	2	0	16	9	8.00	-	-	21	0	-	-	-	-		
H.F.Willcocks	1908	1913	13	20	6	186	40	13.28	-	-	619	25	24.76	4-52	-	-	3	
E.K.Willett	1897		3	3	1	112	82*	56.00	-	1							3	
C.D.Williams	1949		4	7	1	234	72	39.00	-	2	270	14	19.28	6-95	1	-		
D.M.Williams	2001	2003	2	3	0	14	14	4.66	-	-							1	
D.S.Williams	1958		2	4	0	80	35	20.00	-	-							2	
G.E.Williams	1908	1909	5	10	0	120	27	12.00	-	-	154	5	30.80	3-96	-	-	2	
R.A.Williams	1897	1904	21	36	0	1222	154	33.94	3	6	1950	95	20.52	10-129	7	5	21	
N.J.Wilton	2002		5	8	1	278	79	39.71	-	2							16	2

	First	Last	M	I	NO	Runs	HS	Avg	100	50	Runs	Wkts	Avg	Best	5i	10m	ct	st
A.E.Winter	1927		4	5	0	56	29	11.20	-	-	79	3	26.33	2-17	-	-	6	1
P.J.Withers	1957	1958	2	3	1	2	2	1.00	-	-	265	8	33.12	3-13	-	-	-	-
P.A.S.Wollocombe	1947	1949	6	7	1	192	76	32.00	-	1		0	-	-	-	-	8	-
R.H.Wollocombe	1950		4	7	1	143	46	23.83	-	-	84	0	-	-	-	-	-	-
A.V.G.Wolton	1939		7	11	1	245	57	24.50	-	1	65	2	32.50	1-12	-	-	3	-
J.R.Wood	1994	2006	66	117	9	3842	220*	35.57	7	18	1372	45	30.48	4-49	-	-	45	-
W.Y.Woodburn	1910	1937	184	264	38	3987	120	17.64	1	15	10773	549	19.62	7-53	32	5	124	1
A.J.Woodroffe	1969	1970	2	4	0	2	2	0.50	-	-							1	
S.J.Woodward	2008		2	4	3	84	30	21.00	-	-							1	
J.A.Woolhead	1980	1987	17	26	3	450	87	19.56	-	1	213	5	42.60	2-11	-	-	6	-
A.F.Woollett	1958		3	6	0	87	51	14.50	-	1							1	
A.W.Woolley	1933	1934	8	12	2	197	45	19.70	-	-							2	-
H.M.Worsley	1899	1900	7	12	1	210	52	19.09	-	1	130	5	26.00	2-26	-	-	3	-
J.Wort	1946		1	2	0	2	1	1.00	-	-							-	
C.F.Wright	2003		1	1	0	1	1*	-	-	-							1	
W.S.Wright	1904		1	2	0	27	27	13.50	-	-	40	2	20.00	2-40	-	-	-	-
J.F.Wyatt	1964	1965	8	14	0	157	40	11.21	-	-	0	0	-	-	-	-	4	-
S.J.Wyatt	2001	2002	10	16	1	297	84*	19.80	-	2							5	-
C.T.Wynyard	1912		4	7	0	99	53	14.14	-	1	108	3	36.00	1-10	-	-	-	-
J.A.Yates	1900		3	6	1	12	7	2.40	-	-							1	-
D.E.Young	1953	1959	49	76	8	1234	70	18.14	-	3	2117	79	26.79	5-12	2	-	31	-
Young	1900		1	2	1	0	0*	0.00	-	-	24	0	-	-	-	-	-	-

Note: The OW column denotes wickets taken in innings where no bowling analyses are available. These wickets are ignored when working out the bowling average.

CAMBRIDGESHIRE CRICKETERS
(Published 2007)

Amendments to 28th September 2008

Page	
3	End of 4th paragraph should read reformed 17th February 1866
	Delete between 1866 and 1868
6	WEL Bayliff Club: Bishops Stortford
	GJ Boudier Club: Audley End
7	GS Davies should be Gerald not George
8	AJD Diver delete Uncle of EJ
	AA Farmer Club: Lincoln's Inn
	FP Fenner step-brother of J and G
	F French Club: Cambridge Victoria
9	WJS Hammersley Club: Bury St Edmunds
	GF Helm b 11.1.1838
	AM Hoare Club: Audley End
11	W Mills Club: Audley End
	JG Nash Also Hertfordshire
	WHL Pattisson Club: Epping
12	FC Pryor Club: Cambridge Victoria
	M Seymour c not b 22.3.1835
	Smith could be W Club: March
16	JDR Benson delete son of MR
17	AH Bristowe delete Arthur Hilary
21	EJ Diver delete nephew of AJ
23	BJ Gambrell d 5.2.2008 Ringstead, Northamptonshire
28	E Laurie b 23.1.1883. d 26.12.1939 Cambridge
	DRC Law delete Charles
29	DR Lutton b Belfast, Northern Ireland. rhb
30	EC Marchant ed CU (St John's) not Peterhouse
36	P Antony Shippey
	DJ Smallwood ed CU (St John's)
37	JA Sunshine b Southwark, Surrey
	MDR Sutliff
38	PA Swannell
	AF Thomas amend to ALAN FRANCIS THOMAS b 7.4.1910 Isleworth, Middlesex
	Club: Bomber Command
39	H Wale Also Northumberland
40	DD Weekes b Montserrat. rhb. lb
41	J David Williams
50	TW Brown first line should be MC and second line All
57	CGE Jones should be line below All 1900
	C Jones MC 1998-2006